SRINAGAR

SRINAGAR
an architectural legacy

Feisal Alkazi

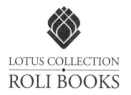

LOTUS COLLECTION
ROLI BOOKS

PHOTO CREDITS

Alkazi Foundation: Pages 12, 13, 15, 18, 41.
British Library: Pages 24, 26, 48, 60, 65, 73, 85, 87.
Corbis: Pages 8-9.
INTACH (Srinagar Chapter): Pages 23, 98, 116, 120, 124-125, 134-135, 150-151, 156, 157, 162-163, 169, 172-173, 175, 182-183.
Jatinder Marwaha: Pages 6, 17, 53, 69, 71, 77, 78-79, 89, 91, 97, 101, 103, 110, 137, 138, 151, 153, 155, 158, 178, 181, 187, 197, 207, 208.
Maqsood Bhat: Pages 11, 112, 165, 177, 193, 194.
Priti Jain: Pages 14, 20, 25, 29, 31, 35, 37, 45, 47, 51, 54, 56, 81, 92, 95, 105, 107, 109, 114-115, 117, 119, 122, 124, 126, 128, 131, 132, 142, 144, 171, 198, 201, 204.
Sajad Safeeq: Pages 59, 63, 75, 82, 140, 148, 173, 183, 185.

Front Cover: Khanqah-i-Mualla, mosque dedicated to Shah Hamadan. Pius Lee/Shutterstock.com.
Back Cover: Elevation of one of the pavilions in the Shalimar Gardens, INTACH.

Lotus Collection

© INTACH, 2014

First published in 2014
Second Impression, 2015
The Lotus Collection
An imprint of
Roli Books Pvt. Ltd.
M-75, G.K. II Market
New Delhi 110 048
Phone: ++91-011-40682000
Fax: ++91-11-2921 7185
E-mail: info@rolibooks.com
Website: www.rolibooks.com
Also at
Bengaluru, Chennai, and Mumbai

Design: Bonita Vaz-Shimray
Cover: Sneha Pamneja

ISBN: 978-81-7436-918-5

Printed at Rakmo Press, New Delhi

Contents

Acknowledgements

This book would have been impossible without the unstinted cooperation of Saleem Beg and Sameer Hamadani from the Srinagar chapter of INTACH. I am especially grateful to Sameer for taking me on several of the walks featured here and sharing his extensive knowledge of all things Kashmiri! In addition, both Saima Iqbal of INTACH who introduced me to the unexplored vistas of the old city in 2006, and Abid Hussain, also of INTACH, who provided much logistical support have been of great help. This book is based on the extensive listing carried out in 2004 by the team of Sameer, Abid, Saima, and Jabeen.

In Delhi, Shobita Punja of INTACH has been a great support all the way through. Finally, I would like to thank Ratna Mathur who introduced me to this engaging city in 2003 and suggested that I initiate a heritage education project on the city, that was finally carried out in 2006 and became a separate book *Discovering Kashmir*, released in May 2009 in Srinagar.

Any work on Kashmir would have been impossible without the support of my long-time colleague Priti Jain who has also contributed some of the photographs in this publication. Most of the other photos are by Jatinder Marwaha. The 19th-century photographs are courtesy the Alkazi Collection of Photography. Finally, without Mr. Hamza this book would have never seen the light of day. Thanks.

Feisal Alkazi
January, 2014

Facing Page: Nestled among trees, a residential complex is reflected in the serene waters of the Dal Lake.

Following pages: Mentioned as Mahasarit in ancient Sanskrit texts, the precints of the Dal Lake in Srinagar were developed by the Mughals with sprawling gardens and pavilions.

INTRODUCTION

In the interior of the city, narrow lanes with traditional houses.

The world over Kashmir has always been seen as a garden of paradise, scented with fresh fruits and luxuriant blossoms, symbolized by the golden chinar leaf. This is a part of India that we associate with the best living traditions of craft, wonderful cuisine, houseboats and shikaras, rushing mountain streams and snow-clad peaks. It is only over the last twenty odd years (since 1989) that Kashmir has been seen as an arena of conflict.

Today as the Valley and its chief city Srinagar limp back to normalcy, we can once again appreciate that unique tradition of values, craftsmanship and an urban culture that this city has personified over the ages.

This book on Srinagar's distinctive architectural heritage attempts to place this built tradition in a specific cultural context, where environment and history combined to create a unique style. Looking at several wood and brick homes in the old city with their unusual features of pinjarakari, dubs, khatamband

ceilings and dhajji-diwari construction, one can get a feel of the city as it was hundred years ago. Dotting the city at the time (and even today) were Sufi shrines and distinctive Kashmiri mosques with their pyramidical three-tiered roofs, often planted with tulips, daffodils and narcissus. And in places one would have seen the beginnings of colonial architecture in stone, brick, wood and stucco. The city at the time was linked only by waterways and riverine transport, as there were few roads. Srinagar was home to the constant play of seasons: the heavy snow of winter that trapped everyone indoors, spring with its many blossoms,

British view of a Kashmiri beauty in a traditional pheran, head scarf, and ornaments.

A 19th-century photograph of life on the Jhelum riverbank.

a warm summer – season of fruits and a golden autumn of russet chinars. So as we uncover the layers of Kashmiri architectural heritage we can see a tapestry made up of very different strands.

This book can be used to explore the history and architectural legacy of this 500-year-old city. It is divided into two distinct parts – the first attempts to bring alive the rich past with its alternate eras of sorrow and celebration, and place the style of Kashmiri architecture in a specific context. The second part lays out a series of walks, each of approximately 3–3½ hours duration, that give you a chance to discover the city, book in hand, and get a sense of the architectural heritage, as well as the dynamic interplay of civic life, religion and trade in the city. In the appendices you will find details of a recent, very successful architectural conservation project, the Aali Masjid, and a brief section on the best loved of Kashmiri handicrafts – the shawl, papier-mâché, and woodcarving.

The city at the present is rapidly changing: malls replacing colonial structures, glass and concrete replacing wood, bay windows replacing the dub ... . Much of the beauty of Kashmiri residential architecture can still be seen in

Traditional Gujjar family on the move in the Valley in the 19th century.
Facing Page: Contemporary Gujjars travel across the Valley every summer, talking their flocks of sheep to alpine pastures above the tree line.

several houses around Ali Kadal and Zaina Kadal bridges in the old city, but this is a building tradition that may not survive. Over the past five years, the Srinagar chapter of INTACH (Indian National Trust for Art and Cultural Heritage), on the request of CHEK (Centre for Heritage and Environment of Kashmir) has worked assiduously at documenting this building tradition, covering 838 homes, religious buildings, commercial and administrative complexes, gardens and canals to create an impressive five-volume set of listings. The present book is based entirely on these listings and additional research in the field and in libraries.

The unique architectural heritage of Srinagar is under threat today, and it can easily turn into just any other faceless city, with no reflection of it's surrounding landscape, local building material or indigenous traditions, in much of its contemporary architecture. Fortunately, the city continues to be home to an extraordinary range of social, cultural and economic assets in its traditional knowledge systems, oral traditions, and in the skills of art and craft. It is only by documenting and harnessing these living traditions that steps can be taken to preserve and conserve its unique character.

1
THE CITY OF SRINAGAR

Outside the Sufi shrine of Dastageer Sahib with its traditional
three-tiered roof.

Till today Srinagar continues to be one of India's unique urban centres with a rich living heritage, an ideal environment to study the impact of historical change on art, architecture and history. Its location in the middle of the valley of Kashmir, surrounded by extremely high mountains, has allowed it to develop a unique culture of its own.

The Valley is located at the crossroads of four very different civilizations, each of which had a tremendous impact on its local history. The Indo-Gangetic plain with its imperial capital either in or around Delhi; the civilization of West Asia; Central Asia; including Samarkand and Bukhara, and finally the kingdom of China, through Tibet. Kashmir Valley is also the last sufficiently populated and accessible plain with abundant natural resources before those of Central Asia and the historic Silk Route.

As Srinagar could easily be accessed both by land and water, it emerged first as a trading post and then developed into an urban centre. Trade has always been a major part of the Kashmir story, drawing merchants from far and wide over several centuries.

The mountains of Kashmir surround and safeguard this Valley, and the titanic forces that created this range resulted in an extraordinarily rich and unique eco-system. The fertile plain, well irrigated by several large lakes and the Jhelum River, could easily sustain a large population.

Over the centuries different groups came and settled permanently in the

The Maharaja's boat crosses the water with the city in the background, 19th century.

Valley. The Sakas who arrived in the second century B.C. made the Valley their home as did the Yuechi tribe of China later, from whom Emperor Kanishka emerged. The Huns arrived in the fourth century A.D. and the Gujjars came from North Punjab even later. Similarly, from Tibet, a large number of people regularly migrated into the Valley.

Kashmir was therefore a meeting point for all those coming in through the mountain passes. From Tibet, India, the North West Frontier Province, then the plains of west Punjab (contemporary Pakistan) and also from the Middle East and the coast of the Eastern Mediterranean, right upto Egypt.

> A white foot print set in a mass of black mountains. This is the valley of Kashmir, known to its inhabitants as Kashir. Perched securely among the Himalayas at a mean level of 5200 feet above sea level and a total area of 5000 sq km. North, East and West range after range of mountains guard the valley from the outer world, while on the South it is cut off from the Punjab by rocky barriers fifty to seventy-five miles in width.
>
> **Walter R. Lawrence**
> *The Valley of Kashmir*

The River Jhelum, on whose banks Srinagar developed, was a perennial water source and the most convenient trade and traffic route into the Valley.

Besides, the Valley was well endowed with natural barriers that could easily be defended. The river and Anchar Lake acted as natural boundaries on the north and west, with Dal Lake limiting any expansion to the eastwhile Hari Parbat, and Takht-i-Sulaiman served as natural defining landmarks.

Kashmir also met three other empires that were to greatly influence its history – the empires of religion – Hinduism, Buddhism, and Islam and three linguistic realms: the Indo-European languages, the Dardic languages, and those of Tibet.

Such an isolated jewel, almost like an island of paradise, attracted the priest, the pleasure seeker, and the profiteer.

Founded during the reign of Ashoka in 250 B.C. near Pandrethan, the capital was shifted to the present site of Srinagar around Hari Parbat hillock by Paravasena XI, only in the sixth century. The city was named Parvarpura at the time. It is said to have contained well-built wooden houses, numerous water canals linked to the Jhelum, and well-organized markets.

At different points in its chequered history Srinagar has been a Neolithic settlement, the host city for the fourth international Buddhist Council in the

Traditional construction of a kadal (bridge) across the River Jhelum. In the background the hill of Hari Parbat and in front of it, Khanqah-i-Mualla, the Sufi shrine of Shah Hamadan, 19th century.

second century A.D., the thriving commercial capital of a Hindu kingdom, and witnessed the long reign of the Sultans – who themselves were Buddhist converts to Islam. The city developed on the right bank of the River Jhelum, extending up to Hari Parbat till the fourteenth century.

From sixteenth century onwards a host of outsiders ruled the Valley, some more benign than others. First came the Mughals, making Kashmir an integral part of their vast Indian empire, then the oppressive Afghan and Sikh regimes, and finally the Dogras, and through them, by proxy, the colonial power of the British.

Today we can see layers of different periods and styles that overlap one another, and link Srinagar to other pan-Islamic cities, but it also has a distinct regional flavour, both architecturally and culturally. Isolation in a valley surrounded by extremely high mountains, the harsh climatic conditions (with variations of over 50 degrees in summer and winter temperatures), and, to a large extent, the beliefs of the people, helped in fashioning an urban fabric unlike any other river-based mercantile town in the region.

Jhelum: Lifeline of the Valley

The river is the lifeline of the Valley. The Jhelum was the only means of transportation and internal trade till roads were built in the late nineteenth century. Noiselessly, and majestically the Jhelum glides along the fertile alluvial plain, joined by many tributaries from melting glaciers and nearby mountain streams. Originating from a beautiful spring at Verinag, at the foot of a spur of the Pir Panjal mountains in South-East Kashmir, it follows a hilly track and is a frothy river in its first phase till Anantnag. From Anantnag to Srinagar and onto Sopore, it flows silently through lush green rice fields. At Sopore it flows into the Wular Lake. The lake acts as the river's delta and absorbs its floodwaters. Jhelum then flows out as a tranquil water body very slowly through Baramulla before it enters Pakistan to become one of the famous five rivers of 'panj-ab'.

The river is navigable from Khanabal uptil Baramulla, a distance of 102 kms. This stretch of the river formed the principal highway of Kashmir for the transportation of goods and people before the introduction of motorable roads.

Like most cities that develop on the banks of a river, Srinagar expanded along the meandering course of the Jhelum and the numerous canals linked to it. The riverfront consists of a high stone embankment wall, lined with a series of ghats and dotted with prominent religious buildings like mosques, shrines, khanqahs, and temples. The riverfront also includes prominent civic structures like mohallas, galis and traditional wooden bridges. Lining the riverfront, and in close proximity to one another, are linear stretches of three- to four-storey residential buildings. The traditional riverfront stretches along both the banks of the river from Zero Bridge upto Safa Kadal.

Today, eight centuries later, this riverfront survives as a cohesive, coherent, continuous urban unit, marking the high point of Kashmiri art and culture, and contains outstanding examples of monumental and indigenous architecture. It

Srinagar in 600 AD

From a small cluster of houses crowded on and around Hari Parbat hill, the town of Parvarpura blossomed into a vast sprawling township with habitation, shops, khanqahs, mosques and temples lining both sides of the major S-curve of the Jhelum, in the late Sultanate and Mughal periods. The map given alongside suggests the extent of Shehr-i-Kashmir, as Srinagar was known at the time. The Dal Lake was still far away from the city, unlike today where it forms an important commercial/tourist hub of activity. At the time of the Mughals, the gardens that surround the Dal Lake were approached only by boat, and there were few roads in the city as transportation was largely by water.

The Sher Garhi complex that was built during Afghan rule brought the locus of the city further south, and by the time of the Dogras and of the British (in the 1880s), the Residency was built on one side of the Jhelum, while Raj Bagh and Gogji Bagh were established exactly on the opposite bank; the elite of Srinagar were moving away from the congested old city to the wider expanses of the suburbs. European staff and visitors were initially housed in tents in Chinar Bagh and Sheikh Bagh close to the Residency, but later began to colonize the Dal Lake with their extended stay in houseboats

Today, Srinagar has surrounded the Dal Lake on all sides — the university on one side, and the Sher-i-Kashmir Convention Centre and the Royal Springs Golf Course on the other, leading to the extremely commercialized area of hotels, restaurants, and shops around Dal Gate.

remains one of the most complete and intact settlement patterns of premodern indigenous masonary timber architecture in India.

Though there are other preserved traditional settlements in the world, it is unlikely that there is one which shares this same rich architectural tradition with its extensive medieval narrow streets and pathways linked by navigable water ways.

While the principal symbolic function of Srinagar was always the administrative centre of Kashmir, its survival depended entirely on commerce. It was a city of artisans and dealers, like any other Islamic city of the medieval age. The bazaar and the workshop were the real pulsating centres of the city, which in turn supported an urban, bourgeois lifestyle, centred around men of wealth, of religion, and of letters. It was a trade-based city whose prosperity depended on commerce rather than agriculture.

As in most medieval cities, religion was an important determining factor for the settlement pattern of Srinagar, with most residential quarters clustered around the major khanqahs, shrines or temples. So, in the fourteenth century the city developed around the khanqahs of Bul Bul Shah and Shah Hamdan at Rinchepora (Bul Bul Lanker) and Alauddin Pora (Khanqah-i-Mualla) respectively.

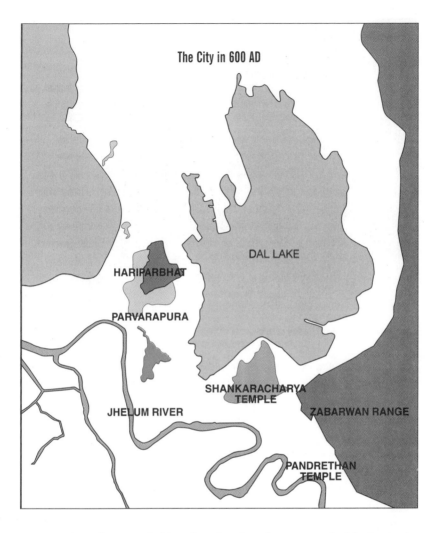

The City in 600 AD

HARIPARBHAT

PARVARAPURA

DAL LAKE

SHANKARACHARYA TEMPLE

JHELUM RIVER

ZABARWAN RANGE

PANDRETHAN TEMPLE

A unique feature of this otherwise densely congested old city is the physical openness around most of the prominent shrines. There is a sense of monumental scale, as these religious structures tower above the surrounding residential quarters. The city was also dotted with smaller mosques and temples which principally served the immediate mohallas that they were a part of. For those temples, mosques or shrines located on the river front, the associated ghat also served as a major urban and social landmark. Over the centuries, as the city continued to expand, the relation between religion and the urban fabric continued to grow.

Carpet weavers at work. A 19th-century painting.

Though located on a river bank, old Srinagar does not open out onto the river. The river front is lined with numerous ghats (steps leading down to the river) on both banks, yet their scale is mostly insignificant. As compared to the holy city of Varanasi, the ghats of Srinagar do not form a continuous linear strip along the riverfront, instead, they are mostly isolated dots located on the banks of the Jhelum at the periphery of the individual mohalla, lane or kucha, with no physical link to one another.

Mixed neighbourhoods were always a part of the overall urban pattern, yet certain mohallas and streets came to be associated with specific communities or occupations.

An individual mohalla was typically made up of thirty or more residential units with an associated mosque or temple. For those mohallas situated on the banks of the river or a canal, an important urban feature would be the ghat. As water-borne travel was the principal mode of transportation until the twentieth century, the ghat served as the main hub for most goods transported into the city. Though the mohalla ghat might be small, yet its social relevance cannot be understated. The ghats acted as the focal point which attracted both Hindus and Muslims at dawn for ablution. It was here that women gathered to draw water, to wash, and, as is evident from certain old photographs, to

A rare masonary bridge that once crossed one of the canals of the Jhelum River, that now does not exist.

pound rice. In addition, the river was used to wash namdahs, ruffle, wazwan utensils, soak wicker before weaving it into baskets.

Parallel to the river, located at the rear of the mohalla was the cart road that served as the secondary line of communication for the city and also as the public face of the settlement. For it was on this road that the bazaar existed. The intersection of this road with the lane coming down from the bridge formed the chowk, a vibrant pulsating centre of city life. It was here that the social, economic and the political ills of the city were discussed on the narrow wooden edge of the shop, penjh. Initially a baker, barber or butcher's shop or the tonga stand was the nucleus of this activity. By the mid-twentieth century an additional feature was the local newsvendor's stand.

Away from the bustle of the bazaar life, within the residences of the traders, various workshops – the karkhana and the tsaat haal burgeoned, where the carpet weaver, the shawl embroider, the papier-mâché artist worked. The workshop was usually a somber place. What relieved the drudgery of daily life, were the songs capturing the distant visions of the poets of yesteryear. It was here that the ancient oral tradition flourished. These workshops, peopled by illiterate craftspeople, served as the real literary saloons of the day. And as children worked along with their parents, they became a living repository of this cultural legacy.

Houses crowded together overlook one of the canals off the Jhelum.

The residences of the wealthy traders and rich landlords, located on the riverfront, stood out from their neighbours, dominating by their sheer size and scale. Several of these would have their own private access to the river. Yet the overall physical character of the mohalla along the riverfront was of a single cohesive unit. Projecting wooden balconies, intricate lattice-work window screens and birch bark roofs, covered with iris and tulips, created a picturesque image of the city till the early twentieth century.

Some of the houses located in mohallas away from the river would be surrounded by large gardens fenced in by mud walls. In case of mohallas which were occupied by members of the same family, the individual compounds of different residences would be interconnected by means of a smaller side door.

As there was hardly any common public or civic open space along the riverfront, more so in the more densely-populated mohallas, the city dwellers evolved a unique tradition of visiting one of Srinagar's beautiful gardens for daylong picnics. Boat sojourns from Bagh-i-Dilawar Khan to the Dal Lake were quite common until the mid-twentieth century. Even more universally celebrated were the spring festivals held at badamwari, or the mulberry feast held at Maisuma.

The open ground at Idgah was also much frequented by the city dwellers, and the numerous urs and festivals held throughout the year provided unique occasions for prayers and festivities. Besides, every Friday, all the men of each community congregated for prayers at the neighbourhood mosque. All these features helped to create a unique urban lifestyle. Till today, a sense of community pervades daily life in Srinagar. Often at street corners in the early morning, families celebrate someone surviving an accident by serving free food. This is usually *tehr* or *dud vigra*, a dish of rice, haldi, and meat that is fed to passersby. After the *qurbani* (sacrifice) at Id, young boys and girls fan out through the neighbourhood, distributing raw meat for cooking.

But these traditional features of city life and fabric began to be challenged by the colonial influences of the late nineteenth and early twentieth century. Western education spelt the end of the traditional maktabs and pathshalas. New architectural features and urban patterns were introduced. For the first time the river front was converted from a purely private residental area into a public domain, when the bundh was constructed along the river front. The importance of home as work place declined with government institutions providing an alternative livelihood away from the home-based handicraft sector. And traditional mohallas also started losing their original character. Men whose forefathers had lived in a particular mohalla for generations were forced to move out. With their dislocation, the network of family and community life, which had held the fibre of the mohalla together, began to unravel. People moved into individual residences, separated from their neighbours in the new suburbs bringing an end to a lifestyle that linked the individual with his community.

Srinagar's journey into modern times has unfortunately been accompanied by a progressive lack of sensitivity towards its rich cultural and architectural heritage. The city has witnessed the large scale demolition of traditional houses, mosques, shrines and picturesque bazaars, accompanied by environmental degradation of the city's water bodies and wetlands. This, along with unplanned developmental schemes, a lack of civic amenities and political strife has torn through much of the historical fabric of the city.

One can assume that the city will remain visually linked to its past for a few more years. Isolated architectural elements and detailing may help in unifying the old with the new. But what is lost and may never be recovered is not the city, or its urban pattern or its architecture but the lifestyle of yesteryear – the way people interacted – the way they behaved, and the real pulse of the city. For every city develops its own culture: a system of learning and values, unique patterns of behaviour and of celebration, images of an ideal type of personality. The heritage of Srinagar is an inheritance as well as a legacy, a culture and also a responsibility.

2
HISTORY
Its Sources, Pre-History and Early History

A trefoil arch at the Sun Temple of Martand, near Anantnag,
built in the 8th century.

Archaeological evidence in the form of tools and utensils, weapons and coins are the material sources of history, and, of these, there are plenty in Srinagar, housed in the excellent Shri Pratap Singh Museum. Written and visual records, court histories, miniature paintings, letters and travellers' accounts also significantly complement our knowledge of life in the past. Beyond these, there are outstanding monuments from the past: Hindu temples like Martand, Buddhist remains, Sultanate structures, the Mughal gardens... .

Kashmir was fortunate in having several chroniclers of its history through the ages. Scholars suggest that a possible reason is Kashmir's age old links with Central Asia and China, both of whom had strong historical traditions.

The most important of the local historians was Kalhana who wrote his *Rajatarangini* (The River of Princes) in 1148-1149 A.D., tracing Kashmiri history back to 1184 B.C. Some of his work is based on an earlier text, the *Nilamat Purana* of the sixth or seventh century A.D. and prevailing traditions, legends and inscriptions of the past.

With the establishment of the Sultanate in Kashmir in 1320 A.D., several intellectuals from Persia and Turkestan poured into the Valley, bringing their own cultures of history writing. After Kalhana, later historians: Jonaraja in 1459, Malik Haidar Chadoora and Khwaja Ahmed Dedmavi, who wrote *Waqyat-i-Kashmir* in 1747, continued the tradition of recording history.

But history is not only a long list of kings and queens; it is also about people and their lives. This was probably best captured in the *vakhyas* (sayings) of the mystic poetess Lad Ded, or the Nurnama of Sheikh Nooruddin. Travellers to the Valley such as the Chinese pilgrim Hiuen Tsang, who lived here for two years in 631 A.D., biographies of Sufi saints, and the detailed descriptions of the *Jahangir Namah* and *Shahjahan Namah* add to our sources.

The Origin of the Kashmiri Language (Kashir)

Studying the roots of the Kashmiri language (Kashir) we can derive that it belongs to the Dardic group of languages, with its origins south of the Pamir mountains of Central Asia. From studying its structure and its vocabulary, its links with the languages of surrounding areas is obvious. In the north Shina (a Dardic language), in the east Balti and Ladki (Tibeto-Burman language), in the west Pahari and Punjabi, and in the south Dogri and Pahari, all of which are Indo-Aryan languages, have influenced Kashir.

Historically, the language has been written in four scripts: Sharada, Devanagari, Arabic, and Roman.

A view of the resplendent Sun Temple at Martand, near Anantnag, built by Lalitaditya (725-753 AD).

The Shri Pratap Singh Museum

Towards the end of the nineteenth century, the historical sites, habitations and artefacts of Kashmir began to be recognized as being representative of the distinct culture of the region.

In March 1898, the Dogra ruler Maharaja Pratap Singh received a memorandum from his younger brother, General Raja Sir Amar Singh, and a European scholar, Captain S.H. Godmerry, proposing to establish a museum in Srinagar that would house exhibits and artefacts from Jammu, Kashmir, Baltistan, and Gilgit. The museum was set up by Sir John Marshal, the Director General of the Archaeological Survey of India in a building located at Lal Mandi, on the left bank of the river Jhelum.

The collection was limited initially to displays of shawls and armory obtained from the Tosh Khana (royal treasury). After the reorganization of the Archaeological Department in 1913, artefacts excavated at Panderenthan, Parihaspora, the capital city founded by Lalitaditya in the first half of the eighth century AD, and Avantipura, established by Avantivarman (855-883 AD), were first exhibited in the museum. This rich endowment forms the centre of the museum's collection. Subsequently a number of other objects, mostly decorative household items, were acquired by the museum from private owners.

Till today this museum is located in the same premises, though a brand new building has come up next door where the entire collection will be soon shifted. The hall is full of beautiful examples of stone and bronze sculpture, including the three-headed Shiva from Panderethan, the delicate rendering of the birth of the Buddha under the branches of a tree and the gorgeous black stone Vishnu sculpture, carved sometime between the eighth and twelfth centuries. Also, one is struck by the remarkable Harwan tiles of the second century AD with images including deer escaping from hunters, dancing figures and hunting scenes. Equally impressive are the fourteenth-century blue and green glazed tiles, redolent of Samarkand.

The collection of Buddhist antiquities from Ladakh consists mainly of unbaked and clay-cast Buddhist seals. With various types of figures of the Buddha, Bodhisattvas, Manjusri, Vajrapani, Tara and a number of other deities.

Entering the adjoining room is almost like stepping into the past for the Natural History section, full of stuffed animals, birds and insects, is reminiscent of a Victorian-era museum. Old specimens of taxidermy fill the glass cases: large jackdaws, huge vultures, herons, snow leopards, snakes in jars, small silver foxes on short legs. Make it a point to look upwards to the tall ceilings and the walls which are painted all over with elaborate designs, for this was originally the state banquet hall of the Maharajas.

And then make your way into the halls of costumes of the people of Kashmir, their textiles and fabrics, and most importantly their shawls. The Kashmiri headdress — the Dastma — worn alike by Muslim peers and Hindu pandits and brocades from England and China are notable here.

The SPS Museum has a rich collection of 59 kani (twill-tapestry) shawls woven from either pashmina or shahtoosh in Kashmir, from the period of the Afghans (1752), to the early decades of Dogra rule (1846–1947). The Museum possesses three outstanding embroidered shawls, and two unique capes or sambosas, all in pashmina and probably from the late-19th century.

Metalwork comes next: samovars (tea containers) of all shapes and sizes, one with a spout like a leopard, a lid like a leopard and even a handle like a leopard! Metal crafts have a long history in Kashmir, both for religious purposes and as decorative and utilitarian objects. The collection of metalwork in the museum includes beaten cooking utensils, trays, aftaba (water jugs), tashtari (wash basins), hukkahs, plates, and tumblers.

Enamelling is a technique of fusing coloured glass onto a metal base by a heating process. In India, this technique is commonly called meenakari. Two extremely fine examples in the museum's collection are the well-preserved flower vases with handles on two sides and a finely engraved trellis design.

Papier-mâché or as it was locally referred to Kar-i-Qalamdaani is also superbly represented in the museum's collection with several large objects.

Paper was introduced into the Valley during the Sultanate period in the late-fourteenth century AD by Sultan Zain-ul Abidin, who sent artisans to Samarkand to learn the art of paper making. Over the ages the tradition of manuscript writing advanced with numerous Arabic and Persian works, either composed or copied for the use of the ruling elite. Additionally, a host of royal libraries established by different Sultans ensured the need for producing copies of books that were considered to be an essential part of the civilized world.

The Manuscript section contains a wide range of objects including books, royal edicts (farmans), deeds etc., dating from the seventeenth century, old Gilgit manuscripts to Sanskrit, Sharada, Persian, Kashmiri, and Arabic works from the nineteenth century. These handwritten manuscripts have been penned on a host of writing materials ranging from the bark of the birch tree (bhoj patra or burza) to fine Kashmiri handmade paper, known in local parlance as koshur kaghaz.

As the Mughal empire came to an end, miniature painters in search of new patrons fanned out across the empire. Many of them moved northwards to form the Pahari, Kangra, and Basohli schools of painting. Beautiful examples of these three schools can be seen in the Painting Gallery. Especially noteworthy are the Kangra miniatures with their characteristic darkened skies heavy with clouds; flying herons; rustling foliage; billowing dupattas; and an omnipresent breeze suggesting a storm that is about to break.

From the Frenchman Franciose Bernier to the Imperial Gazettes written by the British, or in the famous comprehensive volume on Kashmir, *The Valley of Kashmir* by Sir Walter R. Lawrence, many visitors have recorded life in the Valley in detail.

Pre-History

Archaeological evidence suggests that around 3000 B.C. Neolithic man already lived in the Valley – perhaps one place he ever lived in the whole of Asia! Excavations from Burzahom and Gufkral, both located close to Srinagar, establish that over time he developed from being a hunter-gatherer to a pastoralist to finally an agriculturist.

The Neolithic period was an age of self-sufficient village economies. People lived in Burzahom in pits, also in the mountain, accessible by steps or ladders. In these pits archaeologists have found ash (for cooking), animal bones, stone and bone tools. These pits, about a metre deep, could be either square or rectangular in shape. They had dug places for erecting posts in the corners of the pit, which could possibly support a roof.

In the later Megalithic period, the pit walls were plastered with wood and painted red ochre to keep out termites. In one such pit, forty-five post holes have been found suggesting extensive timber and thatched roofs.

Burzahom (located 16 kms north-east of Srinagar) in Kashmiri means home or place of birch. The birch available during that period was at a distance of 24 kms from the pits. It was transported to be used as fuel, as is evident from the ash remains in the pit. Birch bark was also used for thatching of pits, and pine was the major source of timber.

Stone or clay hearths for cooking were placed at the centre of the pit. From the analysis of soil samples we know that Neolithic man consumed wheat, barley and lentils (*dal*).

Many fragments of pottery in the form of bowls, jars, plates, stands, painted pots, and tools such as axes, wedges, chisels, hoes, picks, have also been excavated. Bone tools – such as needles, weapons and arrowheads show a sophistication of technology. Bones of domestic dogs and sheep, goats and buffaloes, along with those of wolves, pigs, Kashmiri stag, Nilgai, and the Himalyan ibex have also been found. These bones have marks of cutting and skinning, indicating that they were killed for food.

Human burials were made in egg-shaped oval pits, with the skeleton found usually in a crouched position. Ten human skeletons have been found thus far – five males, three females, a teenager, and a child.

Facing page: A small temple on the Jhelum riverfront surrounded by residential structures.

A fascinating aspect of burials here is that much like in other cultures, most typically Egypt, animals such as dogs were often buried along with their owners. As in the case of human beings, animals were also buried under the floor of the actual dwelling.

An interesting find at this site is a slab depicting a hunting scene. It depicts an antlered deer being pierced from behind with a long spear by a hunter, and an arrow being discharged from a hunter in front. A hunting dog can also be seen.

Gufkral, located 41 kms south-east of Srinagar, is another important site from the Neolithic and Megalithic period. Guf means cave in Kashmiri and kral means potter, i.e., cave of the potters. The settlements here are round and rectangular in shape, have floors made of red ochre (possibly as a deterrent to termites), and some walls are plastered with mud over reeds. Storage pits have been found in the floor of these homes, containing bone and stone tools. In a later period, those living in this same settlement knew the art of pottery, and had moved from being hunters to being farmers. Beautiful circular hearths and ovens mark later habitation. Terracotta bangles have also been excavated. Evidence has been found that indicates direct links with not only the Harappan civilization, but also with the people of North China and Central Asia.

Early History

Kalhana's *Rajtarangini* suggests that Kashmir formed part of both the Maurayan and Kushan empires. It was also the fountain head of Buddhism for more than a thousand years. It is universally accepted that Kashmir left an indelible mark on the religious and cultural landscape of Tibet, Central Asia, and China. It was through Kashmir that Buddhism travelled on the Silk Route and was welcomed by the Tang Dynasty in China, then to Mongolia and finally arrived in its most easterly home, Japan. By the sixth century A.D., Harwan, on the outskirts of Srinagar, evolved into a great centre of Buddhism. The official records of the Archaeological Survey of India, state that the epoch-making fourth Buddhist Council was held during the reign of the Kushan king Kanishk at Harwan. At this conference held during second century A.D., Buddhism split into the Hinayana and Mahayana sects. The more orthodox was the Hinayana, while the Mahayana (the greater vehicle) accepted new ideas. Mahayana Buddhism later spread across India, Central Asia, Tibet, China, and Japan.

However, by the fourth century A.D. Shaivism emerged as the dominant religion in the Valley, and was to remain so till the twelfth century. Kashmiri Shaivism provides an extremely rich and detailed understanding of the human psyche, and a clear and distinct path of kundalini-siddha yoga to the goal of self realization. Much emphasis is put on personal meditation and reflection by the devotee and his guidance by a guru. The Kashmir Shaivite is not so much concerned with worshipping a personal God as he is with attaining the transcendental state of Siva consciousness. It was Abhinavagupta whose brilliant and encyclopedic

One of the beautiful relief carvings at Martand.

works established Kashmir Shaivism as an important philosophical school. Despite many renowned gurus, the geographic isolation of the Kashmir Valley and later Muslim domination kept the following relatively small.

Four major Chinese pilgrims travelled to India to visit the home of the Buddhist Hiuen Tsang (Xuan-Zang in Chinese). They entered India with a great deal of secrecy as China's borders were sealed in 631 A.D. He stayed in India for ten years, of which two were spent in Buddhist monasteries in Kashmir. He has left a detailed picture of life in the Valley at the time.

Hiuen Tsang stayed in Srinagar at Jainander Vihara which he mentions as a flourishing centre of Buddhism. Pandrethan was also a major centre of Buddhism, and remained so, even after this great religion ceased to be a part of the Valley, around the tenth century.

KSHEMENDRA'S KASHMIR

Kshemendra, a celebrated writer in classical Sanskrit from eleventh century Kashmir, creates a vivid picture of Kashmir.

His novel *Samay Matrika* depicts a vibrant and diverse society. Chiefly urban, it is also relatively stable and harmonious. Its mix is liberal, ranging from busy courtesans to the affluent and the indigent, from intellectuals and workers to the upper crust and the humble classes. There is, for example, a minister seeking religious ordination, a rich moneylender trying to ward off supplicants, and a porter who carries loads along the trade route to the plains. There are priests who resell temple offerings, monks who break their vows on the quiet and doctors who may be quacks. There is an elaborate functioning administration, though some officials make fortunes during the time of autumn harvest, when tax is collected, and others are susceptible to bribery in the court. On one hand, there are country magnates of substance and retired knights, cavalry officers and poets, accountants and shopkeepers, and on the other, there are modest flower sellers on the streets, vendors of liquor, beggars and bandits.

Women move about freely in this society. They inherit property and litigate in courts. The heroine is a rich cattle owner at one time and the respectable widow of a gentleman at another. She is also, in turn, a roadside mendicant's companion, a living goddess and a soothsayer. Her career displays an awareness of the world outside Kashmir. The story refers to Turkish and Chinese people apart from those of Gauda and Vanga of the east India plains. There is mention of the great cities of Varanasi and Pataliputra and of the west Indian kingdom of Malava, whose ruler is represented as maintaining an envoy in the Valley.

A.N.D. Haksar *The Courtesan's Keeper*

The most significant archaeological find of the Buddhist period is the sculpture of Mahamaya (Mother of Buddha) along with her sisters. Kashmiri scholars claim that the ear ornaments worn by her closely resemble the *dehjaru*, worn by married Kashmiri Pandit women till today. This city was destroyed in 960 A.D. by a devastating fire. The most important dynasty to rule in Kashmir before 1000 A.D. was that of the Karkotas. Its famous king, Lalitaditya (729–760 A.D.) conquered most of North India and was a great builder. Religious tolerance was a major reason for his success, bringing peace and security to his people.

Bronze casting began in the Valley when he brought back craftspeople from the South. Lalitaditya had a great impact on sculpture and architecture – particularly temple architecture in the Valley. The beautiful Sun Temple of Martand, near Anantnag, is the best example of the architecture of his reign. He is said to have built his capital at Parihaspora, near Baramulla.

The next major Karkota king was Avantivarman (855–833 A.D.) who consolidated the empire. He established the cities of Avantipur and Sopore and revived Sanskrit learning in Kashmir.

For 300 years, from the ninth to the eleventh centuries, intellectual activity was at its peak. These centuries produced poets, saints and other creative men. Bilhana, the great poet and grammarian was born in the eleventh century at Khonmoh, a village near Pandrethan. Though his intellectual accomplishments surfaced later in South India, where he migrated, his Panrethan ancestry is a matter of established historical record. Somadeva, a Kashmiri Brahmin of Saiva sect, wrote the famous *Katha Sarit Sagar* (The Ocean of Stories) and then there was Kshemendra, a poet in 11th century, who wrote abstract verses of the Ramayana and Mahabharata, compiled Jataka tales and wrote sixteen plays, novels, and long poems.

3
ISLAM IN THE MEDIEVAL WORLD

The famous avenue of poplars on the road from Srinagar to Baramulla.

The swift growth of Islam meant that, for the first time since Alexander, the cultures of the world from the Mediterranean to the Indus were unified. By the ninth or tenth century A.D., a traveller could tell, just by what he could see and hear, whether he was in a land ruled and peopled by Muslims. Beyond the king and his dynasty, it was chiefly the merchant and trader, craftsman and the artisan who constantly crossed borders and carried their faith with them. It was as though there were porous borders in the medieval Islamic world. Structural techniques, decorative motifs, ways of embellishment, artisans and architects moved freely across this world.

Urbanization was a key characteristic of Muslim civilization. While no master plan evolved for the development of a city, great attention was paid to water conservation and distribution, the construction of religious and commercial buildings on a large scale and boosting trade. Individual princes and cities across West and Central Asia, the Middle East and Africa attracted business by providing covered markets, caravanserais, and bridges.

From Spain to Central Asia, Kashmir to the rest of India, rulers across the Islamic world were in constant touch. Presents were regularly exchanged, representatives of the Caliph entertained, embassies established and the fast growing elite and middle class in its relentless search for novelty and conspicuous consumption was always on the look out for architectural innovation, exotic craft objects or even to patronize the talented poet or miniature painter. Books were translated, transcribed, illustrated; metal work and pottery in unusual shapes, sizes and finish came into being and textiles from Kashmiri shawls to floor coverings, carpets to namdahs were patronized by the wealthy. Imported craft objects, all created in a similar 'Islamic' style – whether books or metal work, ceramics or textiles were the cultural ambassadors of the time.

Formalized plant forms, geometrical designs and arabesques, calligraphy would appear as easily on a craft object, as on the wall of a building or woven into fabric, as the depiction of human forms was banned in Islam.

The Islamic household, whether in Cairo or Kashmir, had a minimum of furniture, with cloth being the favoured object. Floors were covered by carpets, walls were hung with carpets or cloth, and settees adorned with textiles, while prayers were read on woven mats. An Egyptian historian suggests that the role played by wooden furniture in European houses was here taken by textiles.

Stuffed mattresses and cushions covered the low divans, copper oil lamps were used for lights, samovars for tea, food was served in copper utensils such

as bowls and cups, and copper braziers were used for heat. Till today copperware, however expensive it might be, is the preferred metal in Kashmir.

Medieval Kashmir

In 1320, the Mongols swept into the Valley through the Baramulla pass, bringing the Lohara dynasty to a shuddering stop. Gengis Khan's third son Ogatay (Ögedei), who ruled over considerable parts of Asia, sent his general Zulqadar Khan, known as Dulacha, to conquer the Valley. As the historian Jonaraja described it: 'When the violence caused by the Demon Dulacha ceased, the son found not his father nor did brother meet brother. Kashmir became almost like a region before the creation, a vast field with men without food and full of grass.' For eight months the destruction continued, Kashmiris had either been killed or had escaped into the mountains and the Mongols burnt all the standing crops. Dulacha decided it was time to leave when there was no longer any food available to feed his troops. While he was crossing the Banihal pass, a snowstorm wiped out his entire army.

Historians debate exactly how the Ladakhi Prince Rinchen rose to power, but from every account it has the appearance of a fable. Escaping from the confusion that had gripped the Ladakhi kingdom after Kublai Khan's (of China) death in 1294, Rinchen took refuge in Kashmir. This Ladakhi prince belonged to the Ladakhi ruling family who had been vassals of Kublai Khan. Rinchen found political asylum in the fort of Ramachandra, prime minister to the king of Kashmir, Sahadeva, and soon wrested power from Ramachandra.

Weary of civil war, anarchy and the weak leadership they had experienced over the previous two centuries, the people welcomed Rinchen as their king.

Recognizing that as a Ladakhi he may not get support in the Valley, Rinchen won Ramachandra's son over to his side, giving him the title of Raina and giving him the provinces of Lar and Ladakh as his jagir. He also married Ramachandra's daughter Kota Rani – but then he did the most surprising thing of all, he converted to Islam.

Attracted by the simple and ritual free tenets of Islam, influenced by the Sufi teacher, Bulbul Shah, Rinchen converted, taking the name Sadruddin. He also persuaded his brother-in-law Ravanachandra to convert and built for his spiritual mentor, the Sufi preacher Bulbul Shah, a hospice and a mosque on the banks of the Jhelum. This was the first mosque to be built in Kashmir and though it was burnt later, it was replaced by another smaller mosque. Rinchen's grave near the mosque was discovered in 1909 by A.H. Francke, the well-known Tibetan scholar and archaeologist (for more on this *see pages 187-89*).

As the famous historian Sir Aurel Stein puts it: 'Islam made its way into Kashmir, not by forcible conquest, but by gradual conversion.'

Shahmir and the Sultanate

Islam had entered the Valley with a thousand refugees who were fleeing the rampaging Mongols. And this was to be the pattern over the centuries as Sufi Sheikhs moved into the Valley to find asylum from persecution in West and Central Asia. Already in different parts of India, the Sufi movement had established itself and Islam had been around for 300 years.

At the time, the number of Muslims in Kashmir was very small, a majority of the population still being Hindu. Moreover, in dress, manners, and customs there was nothing to distinguish them from the Hindus. In Ala-u-dinpura for example, there was a temple which was visited every morning both by the Sultan and his Muslim subjects.

Within a few years Shahmir from the Swat valley ascended the throne, taking the title of Shamsuddin, and established the Sultanate dynasty that reached its climax during the reign of the Budshah. This was the name given to Zain-ul-Abidin who came to the throne when he was only 16, and ruled till he was 66 years old. His reign of 50 years was marked by religious tolerance, justice, peace, a tremendous increase in trade, and overall prosperity.

The Glorious Age of Budshah Zain-ul-Abidin

Following the rather strict reign of his father Sultan Sikander, who ruled according to the shariat, or Islamic law, Zain-ul-Abidin's reign was like a breath of fresh air. While Sikander had banned the use of several music instruments, music and the dancing of women, imposed jeziya on non-Muslims, and prohibited the use of the tilak on the forehead of Hindus, Zain-ul-Abidin reversed all these laws. He brought a sense of celebration back into the Valley. Zain saw himself as ruler of all Kashmiris, not only Kashmiri Muslims. Soon after ascending the throne he completely stopped the practice of state sponsored conversion to Islam, the policy of his father, Sikander. In fact, he appointed a Brahmin Pandit, Shriya Bhatt, to improve the position of Hindus in the Valley. He invited many Hindus in exile to return, abolished the jeziya, the cremation tax, and banned cow slaughter. He personally visited Hindu shrines and for five days a year wore the clothes of a mendicant and fed devotees during the festivals. Kashmiri Pandits entered the state administration in large numbers, among them was the historian Jonaraja.

A copy of the Koran in a private museum with beautiful calligraphy.

Zain-ul-Abidin's reign saw a consolidation of the Sultanate Empire. Instead of spending time outside Kashmir to invade new territories, he focused on bringing peace and prosperity to the Valley. By concentrating on the cultural life of the people, introducing arts and crafts from Central Asia into the Valley, promoting music, painting and learning, he created an atmosphere of enlightenment.

By the time of Zain-ul-Abidin, 'culture' had become as important as 'warfare'. Across the Muslim and Mediterranean world kings vied with one another to patronize the best poet or painter. The royal karkhana or workshop also emerged where courtly crafts were created, which then needed to be transported vast distances to be sold. It was the age of the traditional non-agricultural economy which functioned entirely on cottage industries. A king was not only considered great because he was a warrior, but also if he was an aesthete, who fostered and developed the human and natural resources of his kingdom.

Zain-u-Abidin had a deep appreciation for the highly evolved urban culture of Central Asian cities. Legend has it that as a young man Zain had spent seven years as a virtual prisoner in the court of Timur, and had a chance to see, at first hand, the glorious cities and culture of Samarkand and Bukhara develop. Much of what he initiated in Kashmir was based on this earlier experience.

His concepts brought a new kind of influence to the city, building on a Central Asian city tapestry comprising karkhanas, ziarats and hammams. While he initiated the processes of urbanization, Mirza Haider Dughlat, later consolidated them.

After Timur's death, Shahrukh, his son, a great patron of literature and science, sent several scholars and manuscripts to Zain-ul-Abidin. Other governors ruling over Timur's vast empire, regularly exchanged gifts, scholars, learning and literature with the Budshah embassies and gifts were also exchanged with the Sharif of Mecca, rulers of Delhi, Tibet, Gujarat and Egypt while the king of Gwalior, knowing of Zain's interest in music, sent him valuable works on the subject. Attracted by the encouraging atmosphere and patronage offered by Zain-ul-Abidin, prominent intellectuals moved to the Valley: poets, playwrights, philosophers, and artists.

The fine workmanship and high artistic sophistication that marks Kashmiri crafts received their greatest encouragement and development in Zain-ul-Abidin's reign. Aware of the varied crafts traditions available in Samarkand and Bukhara, the king sent two craftspeople to Samarkand to learn the arts of paper making and book binding. On their return, entire villages were given to them as jagirs to help them train others. Till the early seventeenth century, descendants of these craftspeople still lived in these villages, practising their skill.

Mirza Haider Dughlat who became ruler of Kashmir later and during whose reign some of Zain's buildings were still extant, writes 'the Sultan's palace in the capital has 12 storeys some of which contain 50 rooms, halls and corridors. The beauty of all his (Zain's) structures defy description – all who behold them for the first time, bite the finger of astonishment with the teeth of admiration.'

In *Tarikh-i-Rashidi*

Weavers from Khorasan, Iraq and Turkestan introduced the weavers to brush and loom, and the weaving of silk in the Valley. The making of fireworks also developed during the reign. Schools and education establishments were set up, manuscripts in Sanskriti, Persian, Arabic were transcribed and a large library established in Srinagar.

Travelling incognito across his kingdom, in the manner of Haroun-al-Rashid, Zain kept a close watch on his people's welfare. Years of famine and flood saw an immediate royal response. Land records were kept on birch bark, the prices of goods displayed on copper plates,

The tomb of Budshah Zain-ul-Abidin's mother (Budshah's Dumath) in the Mazar-i-Salateen graveyard, with its characteristic brick architecture.

corrupt officials were punished. Budshah also took up many irrigation works (building nine major canals), drained several marshes making the Valley self-sufficient in food.

Only two of the edifices he built have survived, bearing witness to his great talent in designing. One is the tomb of his mother; the other is the mosque of Madani. Historical records tell us that he established Naushehr (new town), now a part of Srinagar, where his officers and courtiers lived. The centerpiece of this new capital was a twelve-storey palace of wood. He also established three new towns – Zainapur, Zainakot, and Zainagir. In Srinagar, the Jamia Masjid begun by his father was completed by him. In Wular Lake he had built a manmade island called Zaina Lank, that habours the ruins of a beautiful palace and a mosque built by him. It was built as the Budshah's private retreat. It is said that he used to visit this exquisite, isolated island for forty days every year, travelling in a flotilla of magnificent boats down the Jhelum, all the way from Srinagar.

Srinagar now came to be known as Sheher-i-Kashmir, 'The City of Kashmir', an obvious acknowledgment of its pre-eminence as the political and

Traditional carpet weavers in the early 20th century.

cultural centre of the region. The city's overall form continued to be an organic, linear development, principally along the River Jhelum, and, later around the numerous water canals and streets. It was during his reign in the fifteenth century that the first permanent bridge at Ala-u-dinpura, known as Zaina Kadal was built. From now onwards the city would develop on both the banks, though the right bank would continue to outgrow its other half.

Another major physical landmark of the Sultan's reign, linked with the urban development of the city, was the construction of the Nallah Mar canal. In addition to providing a second line of communication to the city, the Nallah Mar canal also helped in draining the low-lying marshy areas surrounding the Dal Lake. The canal was bridged by seven arched bridges, lined with shops and associated workshops. Development along the Rainawari canal also took place during Zain-ul-Abidin's reign. The Sultan had fresh water brought from the Sind River into the city through the Lachma Kul. Although Zain-ul-Abidin shifted his capital to Naushehr, the development of the city remained confined principally to an area in between Ali Kadal, Hari Parbat, and Habba Kadal, during the reign of his successors.

Towards the end of the reign of Sultan Zain-ul-Abidin, the Chaks (one of the five clans of Kashmir) captured power. Zain-ul-Abidin drove them out of the Valley, but they returned in 1528 to seize political power. For a decade Babur's maternal uncle Mirza Haider Dughlat ruled over Kashmir, but he was replaced once again by the Chaks. They offered a stubborn resistance to Akbar; and, with the help of the Bambas and Khakas, defeated the first attempt of the Mughals in 1582 to make Kashmir a part of the Mughal empire.

During the reign of Sultan Yusuf Shah, the last independent ruler of Kashmir, the capital was shifted to the left bank of the Jhelum for the first time. The palace, which occupied the area at present housing Shah Mohalla, Tankipora, was protected by a newly-dug moat, Kut Kul, the pseudo canal. Though the moat failed in its defensive purpose, it continues to be used for water transportation.

Under the Sultanate, Kashmir had opened itself up to the world, particularly the extremely vibrant kingdoms of Central Asia. Persian and Central Asian culture enriched life in the Valley resulting in new styles of architecture and music, painting and crafts. Persian replaced Sanskrit as the court language. Till today the impact of this cultural renaissance in medieval Kashmir can be seen in the cuisine, clothes, marriage customs, art, and literature.

4
THE MUGHALS IN THE VALLEY

The entrance to Pathar Masjid, built by the Mughal empress Noor Jahan.

Three thousand stone cutters, mountain miners and splitters of rock, and two thousand diggers to level the ups and downs, prepared the Mughal road for the visit of the Emperor Akbar to Kashmir in 1589. Kashmir had recently become a part of the empire and was to remain so till 1752. And the Mughal Court on the move took six weeks to travel from Akbarabad (Agra) to Srinagar. Here the emperor relaxed, went water-fowling and hunting and watched the saffron fields being harvested in the autumn. He was accompanied by his son Jahangir, whose love for Kashmir would be even more obsessive than his father's. These Kashmiri pilgrimages are celebrated and well documented and successive emperors had gardens made at stopping places along the way. It is a measure of the peace and security that Akbar had established in northern India that he could stay away from the capital for long stretches of time. We must also realize that the Mughals had three capitals: in Agra, Delhi and in Lahore, and that Srinagar was very much en route.

A uniform system of administration across the subcontinent staffed by an all-India cadre of officials (transferred often to prevent nepotism), supported by a progressive land reform and revenue policy, and impeccable secular values held the huge empire together. Such a strong edifice brought political stability for over two hundred years to India (1526–1757). Akbar's revenue minister Todar Mal standardized the land revenue in the Valley, and Akbar made large donations to temples and gifted cows. On his next visit three years later, Akbar celebrated Diwali in the Valley, instructing people to illuminate all the houses along the Jhelum and all the boats on it. He

THE MUGHALS IN THE VALLEY

Until the seventeenth century the Islamicate society was the most expansive society in the Afro-Eurasian hemisphere and had the most influence on other societies. Part of this influence was due to its central location, but also because expressed in it were cosmopolitan and egalitarian pressures in the older and more traditional lands of this society. Islam offered international sophistication, a flexible political framework, creativity, and growth. In the sixteenth century a large proportion of Islamdom was ruled under three large empires – the Ottoman, the Safavi in the fertile crescent, and the Mughal in India. The three treated each other as diplomatic equals.

Marshall G.S. Hodgson

Rethinking World History

An elegant pavilion in the Shalimar gardens built by Mughal Emperor Shah Jahan.

married the daughter of his Kashmiri foe Shams Chak, while his son Jahangir married two other princesses of Kashmir.

But Kashmir was much more than a pleasure garden for the emperor, he knew that by cultivating the goodwill of Kashmiris and the local economy he was securing his border as Kashmir provided direct access to the furthermost northern corner of his empire, Afghanistan.

In several ways the Mughals reintroduced Kashmir to the rest of India – Kashmiri shawls were greatly patronized by Akbar and Kashmiri papier-mâché objects such as pen cases appeared everywhere. Kashmiri flora and fauna were captured by the outstanding miniature painter Mansur and Mughal architecture entered the Valley – reflected both in the strong fortifications of Hari Parbat initiated by Akbar to provide jobs to people during years of famine; and in the Mughal gardens of Shalimar, Nishat, Chasme Shahi among others.

Akbar made three visits to the Valley while it is said his son Jahangir visited it as many as thirteen times.

Akbar's third and last visit in 1597 coincided with a terrible famine. Father Jerome Xavier, a Jesuit priest who accompanied Akbar describes the level of

In the karkhanas at the court of Akbar and Jahangir, Indian craftspeople worked with Persian and Turkish masters, under the enlightened supervision of the Emperors, to create a new, harmonious art and architecture that integrated the best of both great cultures. A fusion that found its architectural epitome in Fatehpur Sikri; its artistic one in the blending of Indian flora and Islamic calligraphy in miniature and marble inlay; just as literacy apotheosis was the creation of the Urdu language.

In crafts, this transfusion created a whole new repertoire of skills and techniques, and a directory of designs and motifs that were both new and unmistakably and uniquely Indian. It also added a new colour palette of turquoise blues, emerald greens, amethyst, lapis, verdian and brilliant white to the traditional Indian saffrons, indigos and vermilion. Great craft traditions of enameling, embroideries, damascene, and inlay workmanship; miniature paintings, glazed ceramic tiles, papier-mâché and metal crafts emerged and still endure recognizably today, despite the erosions caused by British apathy, industrialization, and the loss of the personal patronage under which they flourished.

In mosques, mausoleums, madrassas, palaces and pleasure gardens, the striking new architectural forms were decorated with crafts techniques of all kinds: painted and moulded stuccowork, glazed tiles (in blues and greens and whites that echoed the water, foliage and snows of Islamic paradise) mosaic and mirror-work, fretted geometric jalis, carved marble and inlay work.

The creation of beautiful objects had become, not just an act of worship, but an essential part of man's contribution to his environment. The enjoyment of beauty, its encouragement, and beauty as an integral component of functional design, had itself become a component of culture.
Laila Tyabji

poverty, 'Many mothers were rendered destitute, and having no means of nourishing their children, exposed them for sale in the public places of the city.'

Akbar responded to the famine by providing employment, having a fortification built around the imperial forces stationed at Hari Parbat. The

Facing Page: Kathi Darwaaza on the hill of Hari Parbat built by Mughal Emperor Akbar to provide employment in the famine years.

inscription on the Kathi Darwaza here clearly states that no one was forced to work on the building of Hari Parbat and all were paid. Also that Akbar paid out one crore and nine lakhs of rupees for this construction. 'The very durability of some of the Mughal buildings suggest that the work was paid for. Buildings built by forced, unpaid labour do not last long,' writes Walter Lawrence in *The Valley of Kashmir*.

Pomp, grandeur and ceremony played an essential part in the building of the image of the Mughal Empire. And the Mughal gardens of Kashmir often provided the most appropriate setting. Following Central Asian traditions, large official functions were organized in shamianas (tents) set amidst the opulent greenery, and cascading streams of the Mughal gardens, of which, it is said at the time, there were 777!

> Against the late afternoon lemon sky, a scavenging dragonfly cuts the air while, near enough to touch, a frail butterfly, majestic as a galleon with all sails set, hovers over the festive tulip. Beneath insects and blossoms, an aspiring bud aims skyward, resembling a helium balloon tugging at its cord. Flowers and bud, empowered by their sinuously reaching leaves, become an emblematic silhouette. Mansur's study has overshot – so magnified and lofty – that it carries us above the earth.
>
> **Stuart Cary Welch**
> *Imperial Mughal Painting*

Emperor Jahangir, who succeeded his father, was even more enthralled by the Valley.

Leaving Lahore in March or April, Jahangir and his wife Empress Noor Jahan, would reach the Valley by May. In fact, in the latter years of his reign the joke was that the court was either in Kashmir, travelling to Kashmir, or packing or unpacking from a trip to Kashmir!

'The flowers of Kashmir are beyond counting and calculation,' Jahangir wrote, 'which shall I write of? And how many can I describe?' Many of the flowers he knew of already, such as the varieties of lilies, tulips, narcissus, violet, roses, irises and jasmines, and many others he had to learn or invent names for.

Jahangir spent much of his leisure in travelling about his empire, enjoying the gardens he had built, visiting various historical localities in the plains, and feasting his eyes on mountains. He returned to many of these places repeatedly, often erecting sumptuous summer-houses in the retreats that

Facing page: Pari Mahal in the Zabarwahn mountains, built by Shah Jahan's eldest son Dara Shikoh, overlooking the Dal Lake.

> The whole kingdom wears the appearance of a fertile and highly cultivated garden ... Meadows and vineyards, fields of rice, wheat, hemp, saffron, and many sorts of vegetables, among which are intermingled trenches filled with water, rivulets, canals and several small lakes, vary the enchanting scene. The whole ground is enameled with our European flowers and plants, and covered with our apple, pear, plum, apricot and walnut trees, all bearing fruit in great abundance.
>
> **Francois Bernier**
> *Travels in the Mughal Empire*

pleased him most where he would spend several days. It was Kashmir that had the greatest appeal for this aesthete and where he spent his happiest days.

And with the constant presence of the emperor and his large court Srinagar turned into a meeting point for intellectuals, for poets from Iran, the Mughal court and 'Kashmiris themselves,' all expressing their thoughts in flowery Persian. The lush meadows of the Valley, its snow-capped peaks and calm lakes, were immortalized in beautiful verse. This was the period when the Valley was first likened to a garden, a work of natural beauty that stood out as unique from the rest of its surroundings.

Other than the diaries of the emperors and their distinctive architectural style, we get a vivid picture of Mughal Kashmir from the miniature paintings of Jahangir's time.

It was the custom to have two or three miniature painters always in attendance, attached continually to the emperor's vast entourage. These artists travelled about with the emperor whenever he went on his very frequent tours, in order to transfer to paper any subject in which he showed a special interest.

In one miniature, we see the emperor at the end of the day's march, resting in a garden, one of the many in which the Mughals loved to spend their leisure hours. The painter has depicted the shrubs and trees in full bloom, with birds shyly lingering amidst the blossoms. In the midst, seated on a richly embroidered carpet, the emperor converses with his companion on the delights of his surroundings. In another, he is supervising the construction of a summer-house, discussing with his builder the plan of the pavilion, designing the laying out a garden, fixing the positions of the fountains, cascades, and flower beds.

Although Jahangir in his memoirs mentions over a hundred flower paintings

Mosque built by Dara Shikoh for his spiritual mentor, Mullah Shah on Hari Parbat.

by his chief miniature artist Mansur, only four are extant. Seven varieties of flowers executed on one folio by Mansur bear testimony to the artist's outstanding rendering of natural history.

Jahangir's son Shah Jahan was also enamoured by Kashmir. Brought here for the first time by his father following the death of his mother, Shah Jahan was given the task of designing and building the Shalimar gardens. It was his father-in-law Asaf Khan who built the neighbouring Nishat Garden.

> Without any doubt, this is one of the most favoured spots in the world; or rather it is a combination of the best of all of them, on account of the fresh and bracing climate, the luxuriance of the vegetation and foliage, the abundance of delicious fruits, and the constant succession of lovely gardens and pleasant islands – as well as springs, lakes and cascades. No other kingdom on the face of the globe has yet been discovered by the most experienced traveller that possesses such peculiarly charming features.
>
> – From the *Shah Jahan Nama* of Inayat Khan

Emperor Shah Jahan's oldest and favourite son, Dara Shikoh, was another great

A Mughal miniature painting of the young Prince Salim, later to be Mughal Emperor Jahangir, who was enamoured by Kashmir.

lover of Kashmir who spent many months here along with his spiritual mentor, Mullah Shah. Like his grandfather, Emperor Akbar, Dara Shikoh delighted in the study of religious and sacred texts of the ancient world. The mosque built by Dara Shikoh on Hari Parbat is dedicated to Mullah Shah and is unique, being built in stone rather than in wood. The grey limestone mosque stands in a quiet garden, surrounded by a stone wall. He was also responsible for the building of Pari Mahal. Srinagar offers a rare opportunity to see some of the structures built by Dara Shikoh, as there is nothing left of the ones he built in the plains.

Zafar Khan, one of Shah Jahan's governors in Kashmir, became extremely popular due to his excellent administration, focusing on a liberal approach. A large number of well-known poets and writers, intellectuals and artists flocked to Kashmir as they were sure of patronage here. During this period, Kashmiri artists and calligraphers moved to Delhi to write and illustrate many Mughal manuscripts.

Aurangzeb succeeded Shah Jahan on the throne of Delhi. On Aurangzeb's very first trip to the Valley, along with his sister, Roshan Ara, an accident occurred. An elephant panicked while crossing the Pir Panjal range, and, as a result, a number of elephants and women were killed. Aurangzeb saw this as an ill-omen and decided never to return to the Valley.

In 1700, towards the end of his reign, a significant event occurred that continued to hold special meaning for later generations of Kashmiris. A strand of the beard of Prophet Muhammad, the Moi-i-Muqaddas, was brought by a wealthy Kashmiri merchant to Kashmir. Originally displayed in the Khanqah

Naqshband and then at Hazratbal, the Lake of Hazrat, or the Prophet.

Fourteen governors reigned over Kashmir during Aurangzeb's forty-nine years on the throne of Delhi. His punishing rule and the war of succession that followed his death in 1707 led to the steady decline of Mughal rule in Kashmir. But the Valley still delighted the occasional foreigner who passed by. On his way to Tibet the missionary Ippolito Desideri reached Srinagar in 1714 and describes the town as,

> Standing in wide and most pleasant plain surrounded on all sides by high mountains and densely populated by both Muhammadans and pagans. A big river flows through the middle of the city, and nearby are large and beautiful lakes, whereon, with much pleasure and amusement, one can sail in small boats or in well-found larger vessels. A great many delightful gardens near or on the borders of these lakes form, as it were, a most ornamental garland round the city.

The end of the sultanate and advent of Mughal rule had not affected the settlement pattern of the city. However, Nagar Nagar, the Mughal city they created around Hari Parbat, remained out of bounds for the common city dwellers. From the many structures built by the Mughals in the Valley, the only ones to survive are the Patthar Masjid built by Empress Noor Jahan, the Mullah Shah Complex erected by Dara Shikoh, two gateways on the Hari Parbat hill, and most importantly the exquisite Mughal Gardens that encircle the Dal Lake. The decline of Mughal rule had a disastrous impact on the life and character of the city leading to its visible downfall.

5
THE AFGHANS, THE SIKHS AND THE DOGRAS

Royal samadhi of the Dogra rulers.

Within the next century (1752-1846) two extremely oppressive regimes ruled over the Valley. First came the Afghans, of whom a local poet wrote *'Sir buridan pesh in sangin dilan gulchidan ast'*. Describing the brutality of the Afghan rulers, the writer says that they thought no more of cutting off heads than of plucking a flower.

Twenty-two different governors ruled over Kashmir in the sixty-seven years of Afghan rule. As a result, Afghan rule proved to be a very negative episode in Kashmiri history.

While the Mughals had taken one-third of the produce as revenue for the state, under the Afghans this increased to half. As in other parts of India at the time, jagirdari rights (rights to collect land revenue) were auctioned off to the highest bidder resulting in further exploitation of the peasantry. Forced free labour or begar was reintroduced in the Afghan period, a practice that Emperor Akbar had banned. The change from Mughal to Afghan rule in the eighteenth century may be seen as the beginning of decay of the urban fabric.

Above all, the axis of the Mughal Empire – the Grand Trunk Road – was completely redirected by the Afghans. The new route, in the eighteenth century, circumvented Punjab and Delhi, and, from Afghan ruled Kashmir, the caravans could now reach Peshawar and Kabul without touching Sikh territory. Further, the economic and cultural links between Kashmir and Central Asia continued uninterrupted, as did Kashmiri literary activities, which continued to flourish through contact with Central Asia and Persia.

The Afghan governor Amir Khan Jawan Sher was responsible for building the palace-fort complex of Sherghari, the bridge of Amir Kadal, digging the water causeway of Nallah-i-Amir Khan linking Nagin Lake to Khushal Sar-Gil Sar. The nallah provided an alternate route for the flood water of Dal Lake to join the water of the Jhelum above the city limits. Another Afghan governor, Ata Mohammed Khan Barakzai was responsible for constructing a fort on top of Hari Parbat.

Next came the Sikhs under Ranjit Singh. Devastating famines during these years resulted in a quarter of the Kashmiri population either dying of starvation or moving out of the Valley in search of work.

The village where we stopped was half deserted, and the few inhabitants that remained wore the semblance of extreme wretchedness; without some relief or change of system it seems probable that this part of the country will soon be without inhabitants. Yet the soil seemed favourable for rice cultivation, and the crop appeared to have been a good one. The poor people, however, were likely to reap little advantage from their labours

An unusual bridge with residences on it in 19th century Srinagar.

for a group of soldiers were in the village who had sequestered nine-tenths of the grain for their employer.

– William Moorcraft, *Travels in the Himalayan Provinces of Hindustan and the Punjab, in Ladakh and Kashmir, in Peshawar, Kabul, Kunduz and Bokhara,* 1835

The condition of the people went from bad to worse. Early snowfall destroyed the rice crops, leading to years of famine, then came cholera, and finally plague. Thousands died, thousands more left the Valley – the population of Kashmir fell from 8 lakh to 2 lakh by the 1840s. Summing up the Sikh rule, Baron Charles von Hügel wrote: 'After so much conquest, what can remain of originality to these inhabitants of the valley, after so many changes of rulers, each in turn eager to destroy the works of his predecessors?'

After the death of Ranjit Singh in 1830, a mutiny in the Sikh army sent the whole of Punjab into confusion, paving the way for the Dogras to take over the Valley.

The Dogras
'Each hill, each garden, field, each farmer too they sold
A nation for a price, that makes my blood ice-cold'

– Muhammad Iqbal (about the 1846 sale)

While for earlier rulers – the Mughals, the Afghans, the Sikhs – Kashmir was part of a much larger empire, for the Dogras, Kashmir itself was the empire. The fashioning of the Dogra dynasty was thoroughly intertwined with the project of British colonialism in mid-nineteenth century India. Doubtful about their decision to hand over Kashmir, which occupied a strategically critical position, to a minor Hindu Raja from Jammu who also happened to be ruling a Muslim majority population, the British began a policy regarding Kashmir that was geared toward endowing Gulab Singh's dynasty with the ideals of legitimate rule. While the Dogra would be subject to constant scrutiny, Kashmiris became the subjects of a twice-removed situation within colonial rule, with dual loyalties and no clear means of seeking redressal for their grievances.

Chitralekha Zutshi

Languages of Belonging

Maharaja Gulab Singh bought all the hilly and mountainous country situated to the east of Indus, and west of the Ravi from the British for a mere 75 lakhs of rupees. He was a man of great vigour, foresight, and determination. He repressed opposition and crime with an iron fist and was universally feared and respected.

Gulab Singh laid down the economic structure of the Valley whereby the distribution of rice became a monopoly of the state. The government set the price of rice and other commodities and undertook their supply to the city population. Similarly, the Dagh Shawl Department that controlled the taxation and production of shawls was reorganized and brought firmly under the control of the state. The Maharaja died in 1857 and was succeeded by Maharaja Ranbir Singh who ruled from 1858 to 1885. During his reign the various state departments were organized on the pattern of departments as they existed in British India.

The British became suspicious of the Dogras, particularly as their own interest in the affairs of Central Asia increased in the 1870s. This culminated in the establishment of the British Residency and a State Council to run the affairs of the state in 1889.

It was during the years of Maharaja Sir Pratap Singh's rule that the real modernization of the state took place and several progressive reforms carried through. Sir Walter Lawrence carried out the first assessment of the land revenue system on scientific lines. The Jhelum valley road and Banihal Cart road were built, linking the state with the rest of India.

There was development in the means of communication and telegraphs, telephones and post offices were opened in many places. The isolation of Kashmir from the rest of the country was over, and large numbers of people, mostly Europeans began to visit the Valley. There were many efforts made by Englishmen to buy land to build houses which the Maharaja refused to entertain, and this led to the construction of house boats.

A scheme of drainage, reclaiming waste-land and preventing floods by digging flood channels was put into operation in the Valley. Construction of a water reservoir at Harwan and the establishment of an electricity generating plant at Mohra was also undertaken. Two colleges and a large number of educational institutions were established.

The beginning of Sikh and Dogra rule in the nineteenth century also marked the advent of European influences both architecturally as well as culturally (for more on this see the section *The Changing City – 1850*).

After the death of Maharaja Pratap Singh, his nephew Maharaja Sir Hari Singh ascended the throne in 1925. He continued to govern the state till 1950. The birth of political parties and the growth of political consciousness mark this period. But even more important was the liberation of the country from the British yoke in 1947. It was on 28 January 1957 that the Kashmir Constituent Assembly ended the hereditary rule of the Dogra monarchy, exactly one-hundred-and-ten years after its establishment.

6
THE CHANGING CITY:
1850 ONWARDS

A grand building overlooking the Jhelum, possibly a merchant's residence.

In the early 1850s, the initial years of the Dogra rule in Kashmir, Srinagar looked as it had for the past few centuries – a run down medieval town that had developed along a river front with inadequate roads, no drainage of any sort and a complete lack of town planning. The houses were in a neglected and ruinous condition with broken doors or no doors at all, with shattered lattices, windows stopped up with boards, paper, or rags, walls out of the perpendicular and pitched floors threatening to fall.

Apart from cholera, the flooding of the Jhelum and frequent fires in this city of wooden architecture, made life difficult for the inhabitants. In the 1877–79 famine the population got reduced by half (from 1,27,000 to 60,000). From surrounding villages people streamed into Srinagar in search of food.

According to the census of 1891, Srinagar extended for about two miles along the banks of the river. But by 1911, the city extended more than three miles in a curve, occupying an area of 5,139 acres. In 1941 the density of the city was 18,890 per square mile as against 14,870 in 1891. In 1915, the suburbs of Buchwara and Zadibal were included within the limits of the municipality. The municipal limits were further extended during 1921–23 by the addition of the Zunimar tract containing 36 mohallas and the villages of Batmaloo, Baghi Nand Singh, Sonwar, Bonamsar, Shivpora, and Rathpura.

As a result of these extensions, Srinagar expanded rapidly. By 1941, the city extended over an area of about four miles in length and by about two miles in width. In other words, Srinagar extended from Sonwar to Rambagh on the south, to Sowra and Chattabal Weir on the north respectively.

And as the city expanded, it brought within its ambit several villages that had existed for long on its periphery. Losing their land the villagers took to supplying the city with its many needs: milk, fruit and vegetables, domestic labour, factory work, work as coolies or in the expanding transport and tourism trade. While in 1911, domestic labourers were 7 per cent of the wage earners, in 1931 they constituted 18 per cent. Also by 1901, 7000 people were employed in the Srinagar Silk Factory.

1885 is a key date in Srinagar's urban history because the accession of the Dogra ruler Maharaja Pratap Singh saw sweeping changes. During his reign the British Residency began in Srinagar with the Resident living in an elegant mansion. The British flag flew over the Residency, all British officers in the state reported directly to him – and he himself took an active part in the state's administration.

A traditional residence with its characteristic overhanging balcony.

The lifestyle of urban and rural being so markedly different – with an emphasis on private rather than public in the urban, hygiene rather than dirty work habits, resulted in a strong clash and change of values.

The earliest reliable information on rural migration to Srinagar can be obtained from Walter Lawrence's *The Valley of Kashmir*. Lawrence refers to the migration of a large number of villagers to the city during the famine of 1877-79 so as to 'escape from forced labour and to obtain cheap food'. The rural drift is also evident from the fact that, during famines, many villagers were employed on roads by the missionaries.

The presence of a college, schools, hospitals, and hotels in Srinagar meant a new kind of existence for the rural immigrants.

One of these Residents, Colonel Parry Nisbett, greatly improved transport and communication in Kashmir by building the Jhelum Valley Cart Road that reduced the time taken to travel from Baramulla to Srinagar by boat – a twenty-hour journey – to a few hours by road. This road connected Srinagar to the Rawalpindi rail head. Nisbett was also responsible for establishing the first waterworks in the city to supply drinking water to the residents.

In 1911, visitors returning to the city, after an absence of a few years, found many material improvements – new houses, metalled roads, substantial masonary bridges, solid embankments and electric lights. Many of these had been carried out by the Srinagar municipality that had vastly expanded since its establishment in 1886. The inauguration of the land settlement and reorganization of the financial, public works, postal telegraph, and forest departments contributed a great deal to the social and material uplift of the city's inhabitants.

Punjabi traders moved in large numbers into the Valley in 1925, turning Srinagar into even more of a nodal point for the local commercial centres: Baramulla, Islamabad, and Sopore. Domestic trade between these centres resulted in a tremendous mobility of the population.

Most of the Punjabi traders settled in the city permanently or semi-permanently. In Maharaja Bazaar and Maharaj Gunj, the Punjabi businessmen established their trade monopoly which continued till the advent of militancy in 1989. These bazaars were centres for retail, wholesale business and import–export trade. Salt, sugar, tea, tobacco, snuff, seeds, cotton, metals etc., came to these markets mainly from the Punjab.

During the 1920s the population of Kashmir grew by 65.3 per cent. The city of Srinagar itself registered a 22.5 per cent increase in population. A large influx of people from villages to Srinagar, and from elsewhere in India (particularly the Punjab) to Srinagar was the cause for this increase. By 1931 the average number

A 19th-century lithograph with a view of Khanqah-i-Mualla on the Jhelum riverfront.

of people living in each town in the Jhelum Valley was around fifteen compared to 371 in each village. The 1932 census listed several reasons for the growth of towns and rural–urban migration, including the rise of local industries in cities (such as silk manufacture), the transformation of marketplaces into trade centres around villages, and the establishment of an administrative centre in a particular district. These factors, coupled with an increase in wages during the decade, attracted people to towns and urban centres. Furthermore, internal communications improved significantly in this period, reflected in the opening of the Banihal Cart Road, connecting Srinagar with Jammu and other towns of the Punjab such as Lahore and Amritsar. The improvement of internal and external communications gave a fillip to tourism in the main cities of the Valley and the consequent migration of traders from rural to urban areas to hawk their wares.

New centres of trade emerged: Hari Singh High Street, Amira Kadal, and the Residency and the Government Central Market. New shops and offices necessitated the clearing away of buildings that were less profitable and the resident population was pushed back farther and farther from the commercial centre, so such that by 1936 Srinagar was transformed beyond recognition.

7
THE COLONIAL IMPACT

A typical colonial structure from 19th-century Srinagar.

No structure built between 1600-1800 A.D. in any part of the subcontinent could ignore the impact of imperial Mughal architecture. The influence is evident in the layout plan, in elevation, as also in the emphasis on surface decoration and the overall feel in volume, style, and the co-relation of spaces. It was only with the arrival of the British and their completely different world view, expressed most clearly in imperial architecture, that Indian architecture began to change.

The British concept of the city and its civic communities, its focus on health and hygiene, their residential plans – were all at a variance with the existing urban sprawl. Their own architectural styles of this period underwent several changes – but they all drew on an imagined Graeco-Roman past, or from the romantic notion of the quiet and quaint English country cottage. So the sometimes over-ornate decoration of calligraphy, arabesque and geometry, that marks much of the prevailing Indo-Islamic style of surface decoration, gave way to the rather stolid, blank frontage of colonial buildings. The interplay of interior and exterior spaces, whether expressed in the open courtyard, or jaali (lattice work) letting in light (and shadow), garden pavilions, or indeed Mughal gardens themselves were substituted by the complete shutting off of the interior spaces from the exterior. At best the British sahib enjoyed nature from the safety of a closed colonial verandah or a machaan up in a tree. Through the nineteenth century, architecture in Britain, and subsequently in all her colonies, underwent several different stylistic changes.

From 1850 onwards a Public Works Department (PWD) kept track of all government construction in India, and in 1871 a special Royal Engineering College was established to specifically train engineers for the Indian PWD. The dominance of these engineers in government architecture was complete and

> In the nineteenth century, the British in India lifted their eyes up unto the hills – and went there to recover their strength. Before they had really established their rule in India, they had found themselves confined to their enclaves on the coast; they went no further than the adjacent countryside in an attempt to gain some respite from the hot weather. But by the time of Victoria's accession, the British conquest of India had opened up the high hills and the practice of going there was firmly established.
> **Michael Edwardes**
> *Bound to Exile: The Victorians in India*

also much criticized. Most government buildings in India were designed and built by these engineers and till today the PWD department determines government architecture all over India.

The majority of buildings built in Srinagar, during the Dogra period were constructed under the supervision of British engineers and contractors linked to the PWD. As a result most of these buildings on the outside lack any local influence. It is only the interiors that reflect Kashmir's unique character.

British colonialism changed the landscape of India completely. In hitherto unknown areas – Madras (now Chennai), Bombay (now Mumbai), and Calcutta (now Kolkata) were built the three big port towns of India, soon to become among the most important colonial towns of the world. In a similar fashion the British sought out hilly mountain resorts which were developed into hill stations.

A typical Gothic window detail built in the 19th century.

A chain of hill stations emerged across the length and breadth of India – Ooty in the South; Mahabaleshwar and Panchgani near Bombay; Darjeeling not far from Calcutta; and around Delhi were Mussoorie, Dalhousie, Nainital, and the summer capital of British India – Simla. Kashmir, and in particular Srinagar, along with Pahalgam, and Gulmarg were the most admired and sought-after destinations.

In each of these hill station destinations the British sought to recreate something of England. In architectural style, in furnishing and food, in the foliage they planted and in the lifestyle they enjoyed. These hill stations became, in many ways, a home away from home. These country resorts were

A contemporary houseboat on the Dal Lake, similar to those occupied by the British in 19th-century Srinagar. Notice the elaborate walnut wood carving.

also centres where the British government could station troops for the protection of the frontier. They functioned as health resorts, as summer capitals, as centres of social, cultural, and economic production.

Urban development in any hill station (as also in Srinagar) saw the development of a British section of the town which included private residences, religious spaces, and public spaces. The public spaces were the government residences and offices, townhalls, cricket pitches, polo fields, and parks. Religious spaces included the building of churches and the development of graveyards to house their dead. Private spaces included cottages, villas, and bungalows. In Kashmir, the commercial/residential space was the houseboat – a unique institution that came into being because the British could not own

And the first weeks merely confirmed that here was paradise. You luxuriated in the cold air. Your appetite improved. The mutton had a flavour which you did not recollect in India. You praised the vegetables, and fell into ecstasy at the sight of peaches, apples, strawberries, and raspberries, after years of plantains, guavas, and sweet time. You, who could scarcely walk a mile in the low country ... wandered for hours over hill and dale without being fatigued. With what strange sensations of pleasure you threw yourself upon the soft turf bank, and plucked the first daisy which you ever saw out of England! And how you enjoyed the subtropical sensational of sitting over a fire in June!

James Gray
Life in Bombay and the Neighbouring Outstations

property. In addition, commercial spaces like banks, shops, markets came into being as did motorable roads.

The story behind the origin of the houseboats is fascinating. One of the greatest attractions of holidaying in the Valley was picnicking on Dal Lake in boats (doongas). Narain Das, a Kashmiri Pandit, started a small shop to supply the Europeans with essential items. When his shop was destroyed by fire he moved his stores to a doonga, fitting planks to replace the matting walls and roof. When a British officer offered to buy it, Narain Das started building houseboats. The idea was improved upon by many others including Martin Kenard, who in 1918 built the famous two-storey 'Victory'.

A century later, there were estimated to be 500 houseboats on Dal Lake. Since the British were not allowed to own property in Kashmir, it was the only way of finding some form of accommodation. Around the houseboats developed the social and economic life of the Valley. Makers of shawls,

The appeal of 'nature' to the European and in particular to the British was recent; it was only in the late eighteenth and early nineteenth century that more and more members of the leisured class made it the 'fashionable' thing to do.

Observing nature in detail – and going into rhapsody over it – as in the poetry of Wordsworth, Keats and Shelley – coupled with quasi scientific botanical interest was in vogue. There was a dramatic rise of interest about Kashmir in England in 1864 when hundreds of pictures of the Dal Lake in its various moods were published by Samuel Bourne. He was a young bank clerk from Nottingham who, enthused by a local exhibition of photos of Egypt in 1860, moved to India – first sending back photos of Simla in 1863 for publication in the British Journal of Photography and later with his now famous Kashmir series. But even earlier, another pioneer Fredrick Bremner had shot dramatic pictures of Kashmir, positioning it as a 'frontier' space where intrepid imperial adventurers forged into inhospitable terrain.

embroidery, carpets, papier-mâché boxes all benefited from the presence of officers, their wives and children, who arrived in the Valley every summer to escape the heat of the plains.

Other than houseboats on Dal and Nagin lakes, the British often lived in tents set up as camps. For instance, the Chinar Bagh on the Tchuntu Kul Canal is where British bachelors put up. Largely these were army men with the occasional doctor or civil servant. There is a delightful story that a young British woman, intrigued by the seclusion of these bachelors, decided to peep at them, and found nothing of interest! Another possible area for camping was Bagh-e-Dilawar Khan, where the Europeans camped in Dogra times, taking a boat or doonga from there to Dal Lake.

The British could be seen enjoying the forests of Pahalgam, the snows at Gulmarg, taking the air on the promenade around the Dal Lake in Srinagar. As Patrick French writes in his biography of Younghusband (*Younghusband: The Last Great Imperial Adventure*): 'Political officers up from Rajputana rented villas above the Bund and strode the golf links, fresh chaperoned girls wandered through the Mughal Garden with feverish young subalterns.'

Colonial architecture began in Srinagar during Dogra rule in the late nineteenth century. Colleges, factories and hospitals began to be built entirely on western models. Amar Singh College, the Silk Factory, and the Shergarhi Complex are some of the best known examples of this period.

A 19th-century royal houseboat.

Long linear porches that line the entire frontage of the building, double-storied bay windows, corner towers surmounted by octagonal or circular spires, a series of gables and dormers projecting from a steep roof with tall narrow chimneys mark this period of architecture in the Kashmir Valley.

Simultaneously, colonial architectural influences also got assimilated into local residential architecture. Initially it was the elite, directly linked with the Dogra darbar, who patronized this architectural style. Across the entire city one can still find isolated examples of colonial residential buildings, but these are most concentrated in areas like Samadar Bagh, Wazir Bagh, paths of Magarmal Bagh and Karan Nagar. Here one can see till today, cottages, country houses and chalets which would not look out of place anywhere in Europe!

In any city in the world, power gets expressed in terms of landscape. The size and sprawl of buildings and public monuments, contrast with the chawls, tenements and structures that house the poor and the marginalized. In Srinagar we can experience the difference of power wielded by those who live on the south bank of the Jhelum, including Raj Bagh and Gogji Bagh, and those who inhabit the lanes of the old city. While Raj Bagh has tree shaded,

Colonial facade with its repetitive window and arched details.

broad metalled roads with bungalows set back and behind high framed and ornate gates, the houses of the old city drunkenly lean on each other, the rotting timber and old Maharaji bricks naked to the eye. Formal gardens, planted in a certain fashion were set within a fenced off compound. The compound segregated the lives and lifestyles of those in Raj Bagh from those who live directly on the street with limited ventilation and no greenery. Domination is expressed in the bungalow with its definition of space with areas separately designated for living, eating, dining, bathing, and as 'servants quarters'.

The other 'symbolic' landmarks of the colonial town are of course the government buildings. Centres for trade, commerce and administration, cantonments to house the ever increasing army. Till today many public offices are housed in these European style buildings: the district magistrate's headquarters, tax collection offices, law courts, police barracks and jail, post and telegraph offices, banks etc. In addition to these, hotels, colleges, secondary schools, and shops that originally exclusively catered to the colonial customer.

An almost private, secluded world was created where the British could 'camoflague their exile through reassuringly familiar surroundings'. It is said of Calcutta at the time that an English visitor may come and go almost without realizing that he had been to India at all.

Western-style buildings created an environment in which Indians were exposed to European ideas of education, justice, administration, even the post and telegraph system! An Indian student studying the classics, including Shakespeare in English, attended classes in Western-style buildings (the Tyndale Biscoe School in Srinagar), received medical treatment in a Western hospital, mailed a letter from a post office in the Western style and testified in the Sadar Court again under a Western system of justice. Colonialism often expressed itself most completely in architectural terms, and the overriding influence of a British 'environment' on the Indian mind is obvious.

But, to build all these imperial edifices the British had to take recourse to Indian craftspeople. When they arrived in India on the last day of 1599, the style and tools of working on construction or furniture in India were not diametrically different from those in England. However, the rapidly expanding technology of the Industrial Revolution in England, British engineers in India often came across techniques long lost or replaced in England. Manual labour was still very cheap and readily available. Earthwork, for instance, was constructed almost entirely with wicker baskets as the sole means of carriage; yet few countries have built so many massive embankments. Horses, carts, wheelbarrows were rarely used and as for handpumps, steam engines, cranes, steam pile drivers, these were all a distant dream.

However, within the house the touch of indigenous Kashmir became apparent. Silk and woollen carpets on the floor, carved walnut furniture, crewel work curtains and cushion covers all began to enter the Victorian design lexicon – both in India and Europe, where they were exported.

8
SUFISM

A Sufi miniature painting.

Sufism emerged as a reaction to the increasing worldliness of the expanding Muslim community in the Umayad period (661-750 A.D.). The word Sufi itself comes from the word *suf* or wool, a reference to the garments worn by the first 'sufi' mystic – Abu Said. Sufism is a mystical Islamic belief and practice in which Muslims seek to find the truth of divine love through a direct experience of God.

Over time a consensus emerged about the main stages (maqam) on the path. The first stages were those of repentance, a turning away from the sins of the past life, leading to a life of abstinence. The traveller on the path should learn to trust in God, rely upon Him, and patiently wait upon His Will. And then, after a period of fear and hope, there might come a revelation of the divine being – a spiritual awakening in which all objects vanish and there is only God. The human qualities of a traveller who has reached this point would be annihilated, their place was taken by divine qualities: Man and God were united in love. The momentary experience of the divine (marifa) would leave its mark: the soul would be transformed once it returned to the world of everyday life.

It was generally accepted that some human souls were able to walk alone, but for most travellers, it was necessary to accept the teaching and guidance of a sheikh or pir, someone who had advanced further on the path, a master of the spiritual life.

By the eleventh century, those who followed the same master began to identify themselves as a single spiritual family, moving along the same path (tariqa). There was a process of initiation into an order: the taking of an oath of allegiance to the pir or sheikh, the receiving from him of a special cloak, the communication by him of a secret prayer (wird or hizb). In addition to individual prayers, however, there was a ritual which was the central act of the tariqa and the characteristic which marked it as being different to others. This was the dhikr or repetition of the name of Allah, with the intention of turning the soul away from all the distractions of the world and freeing it for the flight towards union with God. The dhikr could take more than one form.

This movement towards union with God was one which affected the emotions as well as the mind and soul, and corresponding to the various stages there might be emotional states or vivid experiences that could be expressed only, if at all, in metaphor or images. Poetry was a major way of realizing God and reams of excellent poetry emerged in Persian, Turkish, Urdu, Sindhi, Pushto, and Punjabi. Today Sufism is often known by the poetry of Jalaluddin Rumi (1207–1273) who wrote in Persian. His epic work *Masnavi* comprises 2600 couplets.

The pir lived in the khanqah built and endowed to him by the princes and nobles, with his family and his professional followers. When the pir died he was succeeded by a khalifa who stood high among the disciples for his moral,

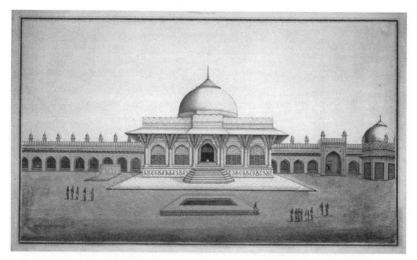

The tomb of Salim Chisthi, a Sufi master, in a courtyard in Fatehpuri Sikri, near Agra.

intellectual, and spiritual qualities. Sometimes, the hereditary principle was followed in making these appointments. The khanqah also had an imam whose duty was to lead the prayers. A living or dead saint could generate worldly power, particularly in the countryside where the absence of organized bureaucratic government allowed the free play of social forces. The residence or tombs of a saint was neutral ground where people could take refuge, and members of different groups who were otherwise distant or hostile could meet to transact business. The saint, or his descendants and the guardians of his tomb, could profit from his reputation of sanctity; offerings from pilgrims would give him wealth and prestige, and they might be called upon to act as arbitrators in dispute.

Over time some of the tombs of saints became the centres of great public liturgical acts. The birthday of the saint, or some day especially associated with him, would be celebrated with a festival during which Muslims and even non-Muslims from the surrounding district or farther would gather to touch the tomb or pray before it and take part in festivities. Some of these gatherings were of only local importance; others would draw visitors from even great distances.

The festival of a saint was also a country fair where goods were bought and sold, and his tomb could be the guardian of a permanent market, or serve as granary for a nomadic tribe.

It was in India that the Sufi order shaped much of Islamic society and profoundly affected the emerging Bhakti Movement.

The Sufis played a key role in spreading Islam in Kashmir.

9
ASPECTS OF ISLAMIC ARCHITECTURE

The entrance to the Jamia Masjid, the main mosque in Srinagar.

Islamic art reached its most eloquent expression in the realm of architecture, particularly the mosque. Within the first few decades of the faith, mosques were established across the entire Islamic world, through the length and breadth of Asia, the Middle East, Africa and large sections of Europe. The English word mosque comes from the Spanish mesquite, a translation of the Arabic term, masjid.

Scholars have suggested that the first mosque at Madina was based on the layout of the Prophet's own house, with cloisters all around a courtyard and the position taken by the Prophet himself when he sat on the truncated palm tree from where he addressed the gathering.

Across the Islamic world all mosques follow the same basic design. An open courtyard leads to a covered space so shaped that long lines of worshippers led by a prayer-leader (imam) can face in the direction of Mecca. A niche (mihrab) marks the wall which they face, and near it is a pulpit (minbar) where a sermon is preached during the noon prayer on Friday. Attached to the building or lying close to it is the minaret (minar) from which the muezzin (mu-adhdhin) calls the faithful to come for prayers five times a day.

> The mosque is not only a religious structure, it serves an even more crucial role as a kind of community centre in which all social, political, educational and individual affairs are transacted.

The forms of Islamic architecture – in particular, the layout plan of the mosque, the tomb and the madrassa (religious school) – already had very clearly defined terms of reference in West Asia between the eighth and the twelfth centuries. Some of these were borrowed from the Roman and Byzantine buildings that already existed there. In Damascus, for instance, the ancient city that soon became the capital of the Islamic empire of the Umayyads from 661 A.D. onwards, the Umayyad mosque had three gates that were earlier part of a Roman temple. It was from ancient Roman towers that the faithful were first called for prayers, and towers began to be used and became what we now recognize as an essential architectural feature of a mosque, the minar.

As most early buildings in West Asia, North Africa and the Mediterranean were built of wood and brick, the architecture reflected how these particular materials could be used. The pointed arch for spanning openings and the half hemisphere of the domed roof.

Facing page: Interior of the Jamia Masjid with its colonnade of pillars.

The first mosque built in India in the 12th century, the Quwwat-ul-Islam mosque near the Qutab Minar in Mehrauli, Delhi.

Beyond the mihrab, a niche that indicates to the Muslim that he is facing the black stone of the Kaaba in Mecca the dome, the minar and the arch are the other features specific to mosque architecture across the world.

It was in Iraq that a new structure in architecture came into being – the hypostyle mosque, a building with a roof resting on rows of columns. Such a structure could be either square or rectangular in shape, and could be made larger or smaller by the addition or subtraction of columns. The mosque at Madina is a pure hypostyle, while in Cordoba in Spain the hypostyle is treated differently with a double row of arches, one upon the other, that supports the vast roof. The hypostyle tradition dominated mosque architecture from 715 A.D. to the tenth century.

As supports for roofs and ceilings, early Islamic architecture used walls and single supports. Most of the columns and capitals were either reused from pre-Islamic buildings or were directly imitated from older models. In the ninth century in Iraq a brick pier was used, a form that spread to Iran and Egypt. Columns and piers were covered with arches.

The majority of early Islamic ceilings were flat. Gabled wooden roofs, however, were erected in the Muslim world west of the Euphrates, and simple barrel vaults to the east. Vaulting, either in brick or in stone, was used, especially in

> The keystone of the arch that stone, or brick placed at the top of the arch which holds it all in place – is the main feature of this technique of spansing an opening. What the arch is actually made of – rubble, stone and brick – has a different significance than when it gets translated into another harder material such as a stone slab cut in the shape of an arch.

secular architecture. Domes were employed frequently in mosques, consistently in mausoleums, and occasionally in secular buildings. Almost all domes are on squinches (supports carried across corners to act as structural transitions to a dome). The most extraordinary use of the squinch occurs in the mausoleum at Tim, where the surface of this structural device is broken into a series of smaller three-dimensional units rearranged into a sort of pyramidal pattern. This rearrangement is the earliest extant example of muqarnas, a stalactite-like decoration that would later be an important element of Islamic architectural ornamentation.

The earliest mosques in India have common architectural features: a straight, flat-roofed chamber, a large courtyard and a delimiting compound wall, with or without cloisters, whose roof is also flat. In place of the truncated palm tree there is now a minbar, where the ulema (clergy) would sit.

Large imposing mosques had already been built in West Asia, but in India the first mosque to be built was the Quwwat-ul-Islam mosque in Mehrauli, a suburb of contemporary Delhi. While in West Asia the qibla (religious orientation of the mosque) was essentially designated by the back wall of the prayer chamber and only had one central mihrab (for over three centuries), in India right from the beginning there was a deliberate multiplication of the mihrab all along the mosque wall.

Mosques were built for varied reasons – the main Jamia Masjid, a few private mosques, those built for royalty as well as for the lay public and an Idgah. An Idgah is typically a large open space in the city with a wall mosque screen, where the vast congregation would assemble on religious days or festivals such as Id.

The Jamia Masjid is a much more ambitious form of building than the neighbourhood mosque as it was built primarily for communal worship every

> In the great classical mosques, the building also contains masqara (a raised platform), a screen or a room for protection of the ruler and dikka, a high platform made of wood or stone, mostly located in the sahn for transmitting the stages of the prayers to the larger congregation.

Friday. The very word 'jami' (from the Arabic root, means 'to assemble') and therefore Jamia Masjid everywhere are built to accommodate hundreds, even thousands of people. Beyond prayer, mosques sometimes become places of pilgrimage or for the administration of justice, as well as providing elementary instruction in the religion.

It was in the fourteenth century in sites such as Tughlakabad, Gaur and Ahmedabad that a uniquely Indian type of Islamic hypostyle mosque was created. In Ahmedabad the Jamia Masjid is a masterly exposition of that style.

In mosques built in earlier periods the external façade was kept completely simple and without any form of decoration, it was the inner walls that expressed the power of belief, with either calligraphy or geometry or arabesque based on flower and vegetable forms becoming the chief inspiration for architectural embellishment across the Islamic world.

The Indian environment, the huge variety of materials with which to build, the specific Indian design sense and the use of indigenous artisans gave Islamic architecture in India a completely different feel.

Elements of the Mosque

The essential elements of a mosque that were established by the time of the early Ummayad rule were:

Mehrab: a niche or a recess in the wall facing the qibla, i.e, Kabba. The wall containing the mehrab was placed perpendicular to an imaginary line pointing in the direction of Kabba and was traditionally devoid of any window openings. In some of the mosques the wall contained a series of clerestory windows, as we can see in Aali Masjid in Srinagar.

Minbar: The pulpit is a stepped platform constructed in situ or a wooden removable structure located to the right of the mehrab. The minber was the only symbolic element in the mosque and was denoted as Minber-i-Nabi (the Prophet's pulpit) in reference to the pulpit from which Prophet Mohammed used to preach.

Hauz and Sahn: The hauz is a small water pool located at the centre of the mosque courtyard (sahn) and used for performing the requisite ablution (wazu). The sahn or courtyard is an essential feature of the main Friday congregational

mosques. An open courtyard with colonnades on three sides that face the main prayer hall on the qibla side, formed the plan of the traditional mosque.

Minar: The minar or the tower served both as an urban landmark and as a place from where the muezzin could make the call for prayers (aazan).

Mosque Architecture in Kashmir

Early Islamic architecture in the Valley was influenced by three different factors – the tradition of building in stone from earlier Hindu and Buddhist times, for example the magnificent Martand temple. Stone was adapted as a building material with very

Interior of a 16th-century mosque in Delhi showing the style of construction and arch details.

slight alteration. There was also an existing indigenous style of wooden architecture, as there was no shortage of wood in Kashmir. Finally, the architecture of Persia and Turkestan, where the medium was usually brick that were further embellished with majolica decorations.

Not surprisingly, however, it was wood that became the preferred material of Muslim Kashmir. The reasons for choosing wood over stone were obvious; namely, the ease of spanning large spaces and the warmth associated with wood in a cold, severe climate. Yet some of the earliest mosques in Kashmir were built in stone; like the mosque at Madin Saheb and Rinchen's mosque. The sahn, minar, and the dome do not feature in this new wooden architectural style.

Every Kashmiri mosque till today has several distinctive features: a large prayer hall that is often double-height, a first floor and a pyramidical roof built in the chaar baam style. This muti-tiered pyramidical roof is surmounted by a

brangh, a square open pavilion used to call the faithful for prayers. The roof is surmounted by a tall pyramidal spire.

Building materials easily available in the Valley greatly determined many of the unique architectural features seen here, as, for example, the extensive use of deodar wood as pillars to support the vast roof of the Jamia Masjid.

The mosques and many other religious buildings like shrines and khanqahs, built during the Sultanate era follow this wooden style of architecture.

This also meant that very regular maintenance of the mosque was required and that it was also prone to extensive damage by fire. The Jamia Masjid in Srinagar for instance suffered great damage after fires in 1479 and 1674, and it was the Mughal Emperor Aurangzeb who undertook its reconstruction. He famously asked if the chinars were safe, for a mosque can be quickly rebuilt but a full-grown chinar cannot be replaced!

The advent of Mughal rule in sixteenth century marked the revival of stone architecture in the Valley in the contemporary Mughal style. The Afghan and especially the Dogra period saw the re-emergence of the traditional wooden style of architecture.

With the advent of the twentieth century, newer forms and materials were introduced in the construction of mosques, drawing inspiration from pan-Islamic influences. The most important building to be rebuilt in this style was the shrine at Hazratbal, which saw the introduction of a dome and a minaret for the first time in Kashmir.

Today, contemporary mosque architecture of Kashmir is a mixture of old and new building elements and styles; only some of them in harmony with their surroundings. Unfortunately, some historical mosques in Kashmir, tracing the Valley's architectural glory, remain ignored or abandoned. Others have been repaired and renovated in a manner that threatens their architectural integrity, while others have been completely demolished and rebuilt.

By the tenth century the mosque was only one of a whole series of expressions of religious faith in architecture. Attached to it you could find madrassas for education, a hall for the dispensation of justice by the qazi, hostels for pilgrims and travellers, hospitals for the sick, and hammams for bathing.

But an even greater cementing factor across the Islamic world were those buildings that drew pilgrims to them – such as the shrines and khanqahs, visited by the community across borders. The Dome of the Rock in Jerusalem, from where the Prophet is said to have ascended, the tomb at Hebron of Abraham, Shia imam shrines, and, most noticeably, the shrines/khanqahs of Sufi mystics are prime examples.

Dastageer Sahib in Srinagar with the characteristic roof of Kashmiri mosque.

Khanqah

In South Asia, the word khanqah and dargah are used interchangeably for Sufi shrines.

A khanqah is a building designed specifically for gatherings of the Sufi brotherhood, or tariqa, and is a place for spiritual retreat and character reformation. In the past, and to a lesser extent nowadays, they often served as hospices for Sufi travellers (salik) and Islamic students (talib). Khanqahs are very often found adjoined to dargahs (shrine of a Sufi saint), mosques and madrassas. They are found throughout the Persian-influenced Islamic world, especially Iran, Central Asia, and South Asia.

The Arabic term Zaawiyah is known in Persian and Urdu as Khanqah. Zaawiyah literally means 'a corner' which denotes the dedication of those who sought the pleasure of Allah by devoting themselves to Him and detaching themselves from the world in a corner. Later, this term became more generalized to denote that place which was dedicated to aid those who sought

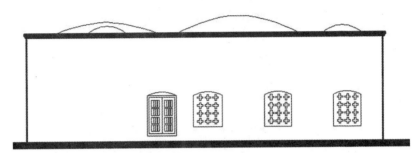

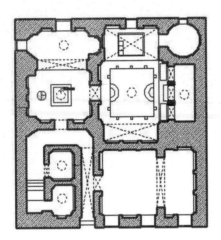

The plan and elevation of Achabal hammam.

reformation and wanted to cleanse themselves of sins.

Hammam

Whoever goes to the bath on forty consecutive Wednesdays will succeed at anything they do.

— Turkish proverb

The idea of a private bathroom in a residential complex is of comparatively recent origin in India. Across the world, right from the ancient worlds of Greeks and Romans, the public baths (or hammam) were an essential part of the city's fabric.

It was the Romans who raised bathing to a fine art, and many Roman baths have been excavated across the Mediterranean. The general scheme consisted of a range of apartments flanking a court. The apodyterium contained niches to serve as lockers. The calidarium had apses for hot baths. Frigidarium or the cold bath was generally a circular room with a large round pool in the centre. There was also an Alipterium where oil massages were carried out. Floors were universally of marble and mosaic. The walls were also sheathed with marble to a considerable height, above which it was stuccoed and painted. The Romans developed a special type of heating in private houses as well as in the baths. Usually accessed from a single entrance, this complex of rooms was always built with extra-thick walls for the conservation of heat. It needed a furnace to heat the water, pipes to carry it and special ventilators to allow the heat to escape.

And as the empire of Rome gave way to the world of Islam, the bathhouse got transformed into the hammam. The hammams built on what had gone before and added to it the Central Asian Turkish tradition of steam bathing, ritual cleansing, and respect of water.

Bath architecture developed with the Ommayad Caliphs and spread across the world. In the Al Hamra in Granada in Spain we find beautiful royal baths, as also in Turkey and Iran. The idea of bathing indoors as opposed to outdoors only came to India with the Mughals. The very first Mughal Emperor Babur writes: 'Three things oppressed us in Hindustan: its heat, its violent winds and dust. Against all three the Bath is a protection.' In the gardens he laid out in Agra, Babur built royal baths.

The hammam survived as the medieval world equivalent of the contemporary sauna and used to house separate chambers for cold and hot baths along with space for masseurs. Within the precinct of royal palaces it developed into a major institution within the harem where important political discussions were held and decisions made. Indeed from the various historical accounts of the reign of the Mughal Emperor Shah Jahan, it became clear that the hammam served as the inner sanctum where only a few privileged intimates of the emperor could gain admittance.

Aside from the royal hammams there were also public bath houses. These were commonly built under royal patronage or as part of an endowment, surrounding caravanserai, mosque, khanqahs etc. Admittance to these public hammams was open to all although in some cases a nominal fee was charged.

Hammams in Srinagar

Conflicting accounts exist regarding who was responsible for introducing the hammam to the Valley. While some historians give credit for this innovation to Sultan Zain-ul-Abidin, others maintain that the Mughal prince Mirza Haider Dughlat was responsible.

The most conclusive argument in favour of Zain-ul-Abidin is his construction of a mausoleum complex (1444 A.D.) near his capital city of Naushehr for the prominent Muslim divine at his court, Syed Mohammed Madani. This complex comprised the tomb of the Syed, a khanqah and a hammam. The hammam has been recently reconstructed by the state government and all archaeological remnants of the old hammam destroyed.

Because of the cold winters of Kashmir, hammams served as major public institutions. Though the rich had their personal hammams, it was the hammams built at mosques and khanqahs that served the general population. By the early 1980s most of the city mosques also had their own hammam. These hammams were open to all free of cost and the maintenance was overseen by the local mohalla or community through contributions.

The earliest trace of a hammam that exists in Kashmir today is at Achabal. Though the garden was laid down by the Mughal Emperor Jahangir, it is not clear whether the hammam formed a part of his original design or is a part of the alterations carried out by his grand-daughter, Jehanara between 1634–1640. Another hammam was built by Shah Jahan at the Shalimar Gardens on the banks of the Dal Lake. The last two surviving examples of a Mughal hammam are from the time of Dara Shikoh, Shah Jahan's eldest son. These consist of a hammam building constructed in the Mullah Shah Mosque complex and another constructed in the foothills of Zabarwan Mountain, within the Pari Mahal complex. Both these complexes are seen as a joint building venture between Dara Shikoh, Jehanara Begum, and Mullah Shah.

Work is on at the present for the conservation and rebuilding of the hammam attached to the caravanserai, just below Mullah Shah's mosque in Srinagar.

The Mughal Gardens

In the same way as Islamic architecture across the world has its own definite style, so does the Islamic garden and entire concept of landscaping. If Islamic architecture – both sacred and secular – constantly brings about an interaction/dialogue between covered and open spaces, Islamic gardening celebrates the interplay of water and greenery. The splashing fountain in the Al-Hamra courtyard in Granada Spain, or the beautiful gardens there; the formal elegance of the central canal that reflects only sections of the Taj Mahal in Agra or the exquisite interplay of height, luxuriant blossom and the sight and sound of running water in the Mughal gardens of Kashmir.

Islamic gardens emerged from the Persian tradition, with its roots as far back as the hanging gardens of Babylon and the terraced gardens of Persepolis. Celebrated in the epic poetry of Firdausi (in the *Shahnama*), Saadi in *Gulistan*, and of course Omar Khayyam.

The Persian garden is essentially a terraced garden – a garden in descending stages with water as one of the principal adornments as well as the very life and soul, the 'raison d'etre' of the garden itself. Water was manipulated beautifully whether as canals or jets of water, waterfalls, cascades, ponds or lakes. Canals and tanks were so constructed as to keep the water brimming to the level of the paths on either side.

Water channel and pavilions in the Shalimar gardens built by Mughal Emperor Shah Jahan.

Each terrace had a char-bagh or four-quartered plan with paved-paths, flower-beds, cypress-avenues and other ornamental features. The Persians adored cypress and plane (chinar) trees the most. Cypress, the evergreen tree, was an ancient symbol of immortality and frequently occurs in Persian art and literature. Plane was preferred for its cool and refreshing shade.

The gardens of Samarkand reflect the prevailing Persian tradition. The architects who planned these gardens came almost invariably from Iran, where Timor (1335–1405 A.D.) laid out many beautiful gardens.

10
TRADITIONAL KASHMIRI RESIDENTIAL ARCHITECTURE

Traditional Kashmiri residence overlooking the Jhelum, with its characteristic over-hanging balcony (dub).

Traditional architecture in Kashmir developed completely in sync with the local environment. Material available in the immediate neighbourhood – grass and birchbark, clay and reed, wood and brick – were used to create a unique style of residence. Most of these materials were absolutely free, and a local building technology, refined over the centuries, led to the building of double-storied structures – structures that could withstand the severe winter and the constant threat of earthquakes.

The indigenous tradition of constructing residences involved the raising of structures of wood and brick on a foundation of stone. The basic structure was a wooden frame, which meant pillars and floors made of wood, with the interior and exterior walls made up of brick. Most buildings were double-storied. While in urban Srinagar we see walls plastered with cement, in rural parts of Kashmir mud plastering is still carried out on walls. These houses often had a shingle or birchbark roofs with a garden of tulips on them.

Rural Architecture

Over a hundred years ago, this is how Walter Lawrence described rural architecture in *The Valley of Kashmir*:

> The Kashmiri village is beautiful in spite of itself. Shaded by the unrivalled plane-tree,
> by walnut, apple and apricot, watered by a clear sparkling stream, the grass banks of

Spring and autumn, when the people remain relatively free from agriculture, are the season when new constructions are usually started. Family priests are invited to lay the foundation of a new house and recite verses from the Holy Quran. Economically well-off families make an offering of a sheep or goat to mark the occasion and the meat of the slaughtered animals is distributed among the relatives and neighbours. People with limited means serve tea to the guests assembled for the occasion. The head mason is presented with a nine-yard piece of muslin cloth to be used by him as a turban. All the skilled as well as unskilled labourers are served dinner on at least two occasions while the construction is in progress. When the building is completed and ready for occupation the priest, relatives, friends, neighbours and the labourers involved in its construction are invited and served with a grand dinner. On this occasion the priest recites verses from the Holy Quran.

Censor Studies *Peoples of India: Jammu and Kashmir*

Traditional rural architecture with an empty hayrick in the foreground.

which are streaked with the coral red of the willow rootlets, surrounded by the tender green of the young rice plant, or the dark, handsome fields of the imbrzal and other rices of the black leaf, the Kashmiri village is rich in natural beauties ... Out through the luxuriant foliage peeps the cultivator's cottage, with its tumble-down, thatched gable roof. Each cottage has a garden plot well stocked with vegetables. Close to the cottage is the wooden granary, an erection like a huge sentry-box, in which the grain is stored, and from which it is taken out by a hole at the bottom. In the courtyard by the cottage the women are busy pounding the rice or maize, and the cotton-spinning wheel is for the time laid aside.

The village enjoys ample room. There is no crowding of houses, and each man's cottage stands within its ring fence of earth, stones or wattling. The earth walls around the garden plots are built in a very simple and ingenious manner. The earth is thrown into a mould formed by wooden planks, and on the top of the earthen slabs thorns are laid, over which more earth is placed. The thorn covering protects the walls against the rain, and the structure will last for some years and is called Des.

The houses are made of unburnt bricks set in wooden frames, and of timber of cedar, pine and fir, the roofs being pointed to throw off snow. In the loft formed by the roof, wood and grass are stored, and the ends are left open to allow these to be thrown out when fire occurs. The thatch is usually of straw. Rice straw is considered to be the best material, but in the vicinity of the lakes, reeds are used. Near the forests the roofs are made of wooden shingles, and the houses are real log huts, the walls being formed of whole logs laid one upon another like the cottages of the Russian peasantry. Further away from the forests the walls are of axe-cut planks fitted into grooved beams. Outside the first floor of the house is a balcony approached by a ladder, where the Kashmiri delights to sit in the summer weather. Later the balcony and the loft are festooned with ropes of dry turnips, apples, maize-cobs for seed, vegetable marrow and chillies, for winter use.

Foundation

Large sections of the old city are built on malyani soil, a black alluvial soil that is good for growing vegetables. This is because some parts of the old city are reclaimed agricultural land and perhaps even earlier were a waterbody (lake) or swamp which was later filled in. Hence there is a need to put down proper foundations before building. A wooden pile foundation is laid approximately 30-40 feet below the surface on which stone is used as a plinth.

Till today, in rural Kashmir, animals are quartered close to living spaces in order to generate heat in the long and cold months of winter. Because of this, ground-floor rooms are built with lower ceilings so that the family can keep warm, while the first floor (where they stay mainly in summer months) have higher ceilings. The ground floor in rural areas consists typically of two rooms – one for the cattle which is unventilated and the other that is used as living/dining/kitchen for the house holders. In summer the living quarters and kitchen move upstairs.

An elaborate four-storied traditional urban structure.

Urban Residential Architecture

The oldest surviving example of traditional architecture in the city of Srinagar dates back to the early nineteenth century. This architectural style that can now only be seen in residences, broadly falls into two distinct categories, depending on the structural system involved. By the early twentieth century, with colonial influence, a newer load-bearing system replaced both these traditional construction systems.

Taq System

In this system of construction, 2.5–3 feet thick brick masonary piers supporting wooden floor beams formed the basic structural system of the building. The distance

---

Dub

One of the most characteristic features of Kashmiri architecture is the dub, a projecting wooden bay window. Located mostly on the upper floors, these were used in the summer months. Square, rectangular or octagonal in plan, the dubs were occasionally provided with window shutters with intricate pinjarakari and delicate mullion work. Some of the dubs were designed as narrow linear galleries running along the length of the entire building.

between two brick piers was usually around 3–4 feet and was known colloquially as a taq. The taq would be filled in with either a window frame or brick masonary of maharaji bricks.

Maharaji bricks are typically 1.5 inches in size, as compared to the British metric brick of 9 x 4 x 3 inches. These bricks can be either sundried or dried in a kiln, and are easily identifiable because of their narrow dimensions. After 1901 these bricks were no longer made in the Valley, so that today, in case they are to be replaced, it poses a problem as contemporary bricks have a different dimension. Mixing maharaji bricks with contemporary bricks makes the frontage ugly, so residents choose to plaster the entire repaired area.

Normally the inner facing of the structure would be made of sun-dried brick (kham seer) or rubble infill. The superstructure usually stood on a 3–4 feet high stone plinth, constructed in random rubble masonary. A series of twin wooden (deodar) tie beams known as das separated the stone masonary from the burnt brick masonary of the superstructure and acted as an isolated diaphragm in between the two layers. The superstructure was therefore a framed structure, which explains how these buildings withstood earthquakes.

An interesting feature of many such buildings is the absence of a truss system supporting the roof. The roof was made of wooden planks resting on wooden rafters. The rafters were in turn supported on a wooden log (nar kooth), running along the entire length of the building. The wooden log was supported on load-bearing masonry piers. Traditionally, Kashmir roofs known as burza pash, consisted of a low-lying pitched roof, covered with burza (layer of birch bark) as a water proofing material. The layer of bark would be covered with soil in which a variety of flowers, including tulips, daffodils and narcissus were planted. From spring onwards these flowers began to bloom bringing an unusual beauty to the city's rooftops. It was only in the beginning of the twentieth century that these traditional roofs were replaced by corrugated G.I. sheet roofs.

This structural system seems to have died out in the early part of twentieth century when load-bearing brick masonry became popular. Also, the manufacture of maharaji bricks stopped.

Dhajji–Dewari

Dhajji-Dewari is the Persian term for a 'patch-quilt wall' traditionally used for construction in Kashmir. This form of construction is also found in Kulu (Kat-ki-kunni) and Uttarakhand (phenol) and involves the placement of wooden beams diagonally, horizontally, and vertically along with bricks. The dhajji-dewari construction is therefore based on a braced-timber framed, structural system, in which 4–9 inches thick masonary is used to fill in the gaps left in between these braces.

These work as shock absorbers at the time of an earthquake, because, along with the soft earth and lime mortar, they impart ductibility, allowing the building to sway rather than shake and tumble. Very few buildings exist in Srinagar today whose construction is based entirely on this system. Often this system was only used to construct the attic (kani) of the building.

Windows with pinjarakari.

Most of the buildings constructed on these two structural systems (taq and dhajji-dewari) have a common spatial arrangement and use of decorative elements.

Many of the smaller traditional buildings are based on a square plan with the main entrance opening onto a centrally located staircase lobby. On both floors one or two rooms lead off the lobby. A part of the lobby on the first floor is usually converted into a smaller room (kuther) over the main entrance on the ground floor. This often includes a projecting wooden bay window (dub). The wooden staircase is constructed as a series of winders and thus the space occupied by it is negligible in comparison with the overall building size. The space underneath the staircase is used as a storage space (ganjeen).

The second floor often consists of a single large hall which can be partitioned into three smaller rooms whenever required with the help of foliated wooden varusis or partition screens. These arched wooden screens covered with beautiful geometrical patterns were either used to partition off large halls into different sections, or the screens could be used as window openings on the external façade.

Located on the first or second floor, the diwan khana where guests would be entertained would consist of a long narrow hall with side galleries

A beautiful khatambandh, ceiling of pine wood panels.

known as *shah-n-sheen* enclosed within wooden varusis on two sides. The hall could be embellished with richly stained wooden columns and varusi with beautifully stenciled walls (naqashi) in bands of blue and dark green on the deep earthy tone of the mud plaster, giving the characteristic rich Kashmiri look.

In many cases, the second floor is surmounted by a cruciform shaped attic space, *briar-kani* (cats crawl) used for storage. In certain cases, the roof itself is surmounted by an open square pavilion, covered with a pyramidal roof known locally as *zoon dub*.

A series of rectangular, square or octagonal wooden bay windows or dubs usually project out of the main façade. In certain cases the clear height of the ground floor would be around 8-9 feet where the upper floors would have higher ceilings. Toilets and bathrooms were provided in a separate building block.

Many of the larger and more aristocratic houses, also know as havelis, have a linear plan and are often two or three-storeys high. These havelis would generally have two or more buildings serving as living quarters (diwan-khana) and sleeping quarters (mahal-khana) aligned around an open courtyard. The entrance to these buildings would be from a staircase usually located in one of the corners of the house. Internally the house would have large halls which could be sub-divided by means of a varusi. In some cases, the house would be connected by a long narrow corridor running at the back along its entire length. Many of these havelis had small Turkish baths or hammams on the ground floor. The courtyards would sometimes be paved with locally available Baramulla stone (paetri).

The main decorative building elements in both the plans remain the same. Lattice work screens (pinjarakari) and window shutters, profusely carved wooden brackets, eaves board (morakh patt), pendants (dour) are some of the main architectural elements.

In some of the larger traditional houses, the ceiling of the hall on the top floor was supported on an arched arcade, resting on top of wooden columns. The arcade would run on all four sides parallel to the wall, creating an open rectangular space in the centre, usually lower than the rest of the surrounding area. The ambulatory space created around this depressed portion was known as ghulam gardish. Similarly, the ambulatory space surrounding the covered central courtyard (pokher) in an imambara was also known as ghulam gardish.

A specialty in Kashmir woodwork are beautiful ceilings in a geometric layout, painstakingly put together by carpenters, who, with marvelous skill, piece together thin panels of pine wood. This is known as khatamband and is said to have been introduced by Mirza Haider Dughlat. Other than the Valley, khatamband is practiced only in Turkey, where it is known as kunde kari. While in Kashmir it is only used for ceilings, in Turkey it is used exclusively for doors and decorative paneling. Possibly this style of geometric wooden decorative work was once widespread across the Islamic world.

Originally known as the Kar-i-qalamdani, the art of papier-mâché is said to have been introduced into Kashmir by Persian and Central Asian craftspeople during the reign of Sultan Zain-ul-Abidin in the fifteenth century. Papier-mâché is made from paper pulp with the naqash or laquer worker painting beautiful designs on the smoothened surface. A few residences in Srinagar still retain their original papier-mâché ceilings. The technique was also used on the door panels and portions of the varusi. The use of papier-mâché was limited to the residences of the richer classes and religious buildings.

The art of applying beautiful floral or geometrical designs on the walls and ceilings of residences was an associated task of the lacquer worker or naqash. This art can be sub-divided into two categories, though the basics remained the same. One was the technique of covering the rendered wall or

Ghulam Gardish and walls decorated with papier-mâché naqashi.
Following pages 114-115: The elaborate façade of Khanqah-i-Mualla, celebrating one of the earliest Sufi masters of the city – Shah Hamadan.

ceiling panel with rogan or lacquer, giving the design a glossy finish. In the other technique, mud plastered walls were covered with designs, the outline of which was stenciled with lime with the patterns themselves being filled with vegetable or natural dyes, predominantly in blue or green.

The Colonial Influence

Indigenous architecture began to change with the first buildings that came up in the Dogra period from 1846, that showed a distinct colonial influence. These influences can be seen in both public as well as residential buildings of the late nineteenth and early twentieth century, when this style found its most visible manifestation. Long linear porches running along the entire length of the building; double-storied bay windows; corner towers surmounted by octagonal or circular spires, a series of gables and dormers projecting from steeply pitched roofs, along with tall, narrow chimneys are some of the most distinct features.

The earliest examples of colonial architecture are the residential quarters for European visitors in Sheikh Bagh and some institutional buildings like

Amar Singh College and the Silk Factory. The Shergarhi Palace Complex which was rebuilt in the nineteenth century, made this architectural style popular among the ruling elite of the state.

Most of the buildings were constructed under the supervision of British engineers or contractors associated with the Public Works Department. The outer walls were without any local influence. It was only in the more decorative and intricate woodwork of the interiors, like khatamband ceilings, eaves board, window pelmets and certain other features that traditional workmanship was used. Within the house there would be a large central lobby opening onto a porch or portico. Rooms continued to be aligned along either side of the staircase lobby as in indigenous houses and most of the rooms were interconnected. Kitchen and other household services (servant's quarters, stores etc.) were generally built away from the main building as annexes. An interesting feature of these houses was the addition of attached toilets to the bedrooms on both floors. Room height was generally 10–12 feet, and gave an airy atmosphere.

This architectural style flourished for around half a century before being modified along contemporary lines.

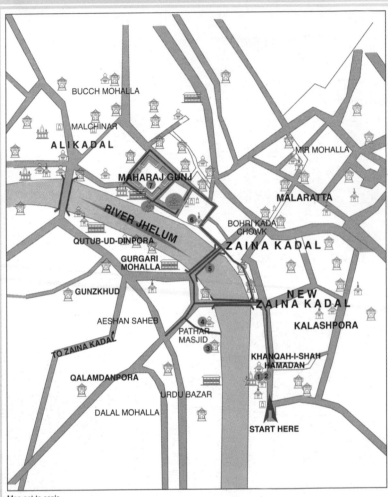

Map not to scale

1 Khanqah-i-Mualla
2 Hammam
3 Mohammad Ramzan Krall's House
4 Pathar Masjid

5 Zaina Kadal Bridge
6 Mazar-i-Salateen
7 Shri Ranbir Gunj Shopping Complex

WALK 1

From Medieval
to Colonial Srinagar

Jhelum riverfront with Khanqah-i-Mualla on the left and
Hari Parbat in the background.

If you have very limited time in the city the two areas not to be missed, and that has a plurality of structures built between the thirteenth and the nineteenth centuries, are the Khanqah-i-Mualla and Maharaj Gunj complex in the oldest part of the city. The place to begin chronologically is the Khanqah-i-Mualla (the Shah Hamdan complex). While this lies on one bank of the Jhelum, almost directly opposite on the other bank stands Pathar Masjid, a building with a chequered history, built by the Mughal Empress Noor Jahan. The oldest wooden bridge in Srinagar, Zaina Kadal, leads the way back across the Jhelum, to the Mazhar-i-Salateen complex, linked to the heyday of the Sultanate and its favourite king, Budshah Zain-ul-Abidin. Around the corner is Maharaj Gunj Ghat, and then the courtyard market of Shri Ranbir Gunj.

 ## KHANQAH-I-MUALLA

Located in a large square in the middle of one of the poorer sections of the old city, the Shah Hamadan complex dates back to the medieval period, and is one of the most important Sufi shrines in the city. The traditional impact of Hamadani is evident in Kashmir in most mosques where, after the first and last prayers the entire congregation recites a compilation of verses by Shah Hamadan.

As you walk towards the main building of the shrine you pass through a grey archway topped by three cupolas (built in the 1960s-70s). But before admiring the main shrine of Khanqah-i-Mualla, look at the large, raised stone platforms (sufa) directly to the right and left of where you are standing. It is said that it was here, seated on these very platforms, that Hamadani began to preach 700 years ago. He was at the time living at an inn in Allaudin Pura (in the immediate vicinity) and it

Hamadani

It was during the Sultanate era that Sayyid Ali Hamadani, one of the most remarkable Sufis of the fourteenth century Islamic world, came to Kashmir. A great scholar in Arabic and Persian, he is said to have been the author of more than one hundred works on logic, jurisprudence, philosophy, political science, ethics and Sufism. Sayyid Ali visited Kashmir several times, the first time in September 1372. In 1383 the Mongol conqueror Timur invaded Persia and decided to exterminate the Alvi Sayyids of Hamadan. Sayyid Ali left Hamadan with 700 Sayyids, and set out for Kashmir to find a safe haven from the wrath of Timur. On hearing the news that Sayyid Ali was approaching Srinagar, Sultan Qutbud-Din went out with his chief officials, received him with great warmth and respect, and escorted him and his followers to the city.

Facing page: Doorway to the shrine with the haankal suspended on three chains.

Elevation of Khanqah-i-Mualla.

was only after his death that his son received a royal grant to erect this khanqah.

The support for maintenance of this shrine used to come from a royal jagir and this is only one of the 30 or 40 odd shrines devoted to Hamadani spread across the Valley. As for Hamadani himself, he was buried in Qulab in Tajikistan. For approximately the first hundred years free food was distributed here in a langar (charity kitchen) to popularize the shrine.

The main building is in plan a square, 70 x 70 feet and is two-storeys tall, which means the eaves are nearly 50 feet above the ground. The pyramidical roof projecting over the whole structure is three-tiered, surmounted by an open pavilion for the muezzin, over which rises the steeple with its finial 125 feet from the ground. Within the building are higher structures such as arcades, verandahs and porticos, their openings filled with lattice work (pinjarakari).

The Khanqah-i-Mualla was twice destroyed by fire, in 1479 and 1731. The present mosque was rebuilt by Abul Barkat Khan in 1732 and since then it has only required occasional repairs.

Over the doorway hangs a metal medallion suspended on three chains. This is a haankal which many believers hold onto and rub before they enter. It is a symbolic representation that the devotee is seeking the support of Hamadani. People come here with their own murads (wishes): the long and healthy life of a squalling infant who they lay in the doorway, good health and happiness for a newly-wed couple... they often carry with them a dash, a piece of cloth they tie to the screen surrounding the relic in the extreme right hand corner. If their murad comes true, they must return to untie it or it is seen as inauspicious.

As you enter the darkened space (where entry is restricted to men) you will see the walls covered with elaborate woodwork in geometric patterns, painted and gilded – almost baroque in their extravagance. Above you hang several chandeliers, all of which are donations and the floor is covered with attractive prayer mats. It is said that Hamadani sat in the right-hand corner. The side chambers in the right and left walls house fourteen chillahs, rooms for solitary meditation. The ceiling is supported by four wooden columns ornamented with wooden pieces in a fishbone pattern. Two painted wooden staircases, one on either side of the entrance door, lead to the higher storey. This is a two-storied structure with each floor by itself being double storied. The birth of Hamadani is a major celebration that draws visitors from across the valley. Dambolis (local dancers) perform a local folk martial dance. It was from here, in 1931, that the populace articulated of the demand for freedom from the Dogra rule.

Walk along the path to your left, as you face the building, to get a closer look at how it has been constructed. Above the 6-feet-high stone plinth, with two narrow bands of carving, starts the wooden structure which also has a similar band of carving. What is amazing is that this entire structure is built entirely of interlocked deodar logs plugged with bricks, where perhaps originally clay was used. This is the traditional style of construction in Kashmir.

Placing one log horizontally on another, usually cross-wise in the form of headers and stretchers, as in brickwork, the walls and also the piers for the support of any superstructure were erected. The logs here are neatly squared and the space between each course filled with brickwork. Consequently it is a system of a dead weight bearing directly downwards, based on the same principles as in the older stone temples in the Valley.

The back of the khanqah building is treated in lime plaster (guch), probably executed in the Sikh period. The entire surface is painted with a variety of designs, the most prominent being stylized flowers in a vase. You

can peep over the railing at the back to see the bright orange marking on the stone just below that suggests a Kali temple. The extension to the rear of the main building allows women to enter for prayer. Directly opposite on the other bank of the Jhelum, behind a recently constructed wall, stands the grey limestone mosque, Pathar Masjid.

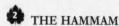 THE HAMMAM

The two-storied hammam building is now directly in front of you. Enter through a small door to see cubicles on your left and right for wazu, the ritual ablution required before entering any mosque for prayer. Climb a flight of stone steps to the first floor where on your right is a square area: the bathing area of the hammam. The middle of the domed central space, with a skylight, is once again for wazu, while the six small bathrooms around the periphery are bathing chambers. The walls are of brick masonary that have been plastered and the floor is completely hollow. On the ground floor, to the right of the building, you can see wood piled in the large hearth used for heating the water for the hammam and keeping the floor and walls warm. With several cold months (November to March) the hammam works daily through winter. It is maintained by a hamami, an employee whose duty it is to light the hearth even before the morning prayers, and keep it going through the day. This is perhaps the oldest surviving hammam in the city, possibly built during the Afghan period.

As you exit the Khanqah-i-Mualla, on your extreme right is a traditional medicine shop, the kozgar, where in the windows you can see glass containers with the distilled essence of various plants.

As you walk out of the Shah Hamadan complex and turn to the left, very soon on your left you will see the new Zaina Kadal Bridge. Cross the Jhelum by this bridge, parallel to the original Zaina Kadal Bridge that you can see on your right. Beyond it you can see the distinctive brick domes of the tomb of Zain-ul-Abidin's mother, which we will visit later on this walk.

MOHAMMED RAMZAN KRALL'S HOUSE

Mohammed Ramzan Krall's house is directly opposite the Khanqah-i-Mualla on the opposite bank. Located at a tremendous vantage point on the river, surrounded by historical religious structures – this well-maintained building is a fine example of Kashmiri residential architecture.

The plan of this two-storied building is U-shaped with the central courtyard giving a clear view of Khanqah-i-Mualla. A timber staircase to the

123

Facing page: The Khanqah-i-Mualla as seen from the river.

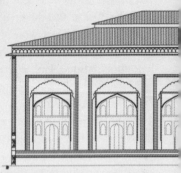

Elevation and the interior of Pathar Masjid,
built by Mughal Empress Noor Jahan.

north of the entrance leads to the first floor, which has a large hall on the entire northern flange of the house. There are three small dubs on the north and a large dub on the east. The hall is very large, around 30 x 20 feet with stained-glass windows and timber pillared interiors. The walls are mud plastered and painted with oil paint. The southern flange of the building also has a large hall which has presently been divided into two. These two halls earlier served as the diwan khana for guests. The house has been redone in some places with marble flooring and cement plaster surfaces; otherwise it is largely in mint condition. Almost all the openings are segmental arches with glazed and panelled window shutters. The ceiling on the ground floor is a plain wooden one, while on the first floor it is an ornate khatamband ceiling.

❹ PATHAR MASJID

But now it is time for Pathar Masjid. Noor Jahan, Mughal empress extraordinaire, who built this particular mosque was the wife of that lover of Kashmir, Jahangir. He was her second husband – and in many respects she was the ruler, even having the distinction of having coins minted in her name. Her family, originally from Persia, had climbed to eminence in the Mughal court. Her father, Itmad-ud-Daula for whom she built an exquisite mausoleum in Agra, served as vazir to Emperor Akbar. Her brother Asaf Khan, who built Nishat Gardens in Srinagar, was Shah Jahan's vazir. Asaf Khan's daughter Mumtaz Mahal was married to the next emperor in waiting, Shah Jahan.

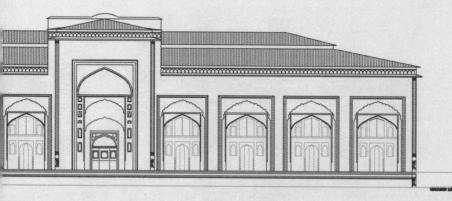

Cross the bridge and turn to your left and you will find yourself walking along the grey limestone wall of Pathar Masjid. Within the courtyard of the mosque, planted with large chinars, lies the mosque itself. Polished limestone as a building material can only be seen here and in Mullah Shah's mosque on Hari Parbhat. Perhaps it was used to state to the Kashmiris that the Mughals were here to stay, and that they built for posterity!

Pathar Masjid is the largest surviving example of fine Mughal architecture in Kashmir. It has a length of 180 feet and a breadth of 51 feet. The façade consists of nine arches, including the large arched portico in the centre. The arched openings are enclosed in shallow decorative cusped arches within rectangular frames. The plinth is surmounted by a lotus-leaf coping.

The frieze between the projecting cornices and the eaves is decorated with a series of large lotus leaves carved in relief. A flight of steps within the door jamb of the entrance gives access to the roof which is, as is usual in Kashmir, sloping, except in the centre, where there was originally a dome, which was later dismantled by the Sikhs. The roof consists of 27 domes, the central one of which is the largest. The domes are mostly ribbed inside, though there are some that are flat or wagon-vaulted.

Unlike most other mosques in the Valley, this building does not have a traditional pyramidical roof. The roof is supported by 18 extraordinarily massive square columns, having projections on two sides. The lower portions of these columns are of stone and the upper portions of brick, covered by a thick layer of buff-coloured lime plaster. The overall style is rather severe, lacking any kind of ornamentation.

The construction of the mosque was supervised by the well-known historian and architect Malik Haider Chadoora. He is also credited with rebuilding the Jamia Masjid, and the khanqah of Mir Shamsud-din Iraqi. He was a very influential landlord, and was close to Emperor Jahangir and Noor

A 19th-century photograph of the area.

Jehan, both of whom had great trust in him. After prolonged agitation by Kashmiris, the mosque was reopened by the Dogra ruler, Maharaja Hari Singh in the late 1930s. On the southern side of the mosque is Mujahid Manzil, headquarters of National Conference since 1934.

5 ZAINA KADAL

As you cross the Jhelum once again, this time on the original Zaina Kadal, built by Zain-ul-Abidin in 1470 (550 years ago!) stop for a minute to look at the two prominent buildings on your left and right. On your left you can see Haji Jaffer Khan's house, now known as Ghani Textile Mills, a grand structure and a wonderful example of Kashmiri architecture. In the pre-independence period this family owned as many as 11 different properties in the Valley. Earlier this property belonged to a family with a flourishing shawl business. In its heyday, the large hall, facing the riverfront was an immense shawl showroom. For more information on the power and economic clout of shawl traders, *see pages* 196-204.

The building is based on the 9 taq system (*see chapter on* Traditional Kashmiri Architecture) and has pointed arch openings with pinjarakari (lattice work). The entire plan of the house is repeated on the upper floor of this two-storied house. The first level has a pair of projecting dubs on the north eastern side, facing the river. The second level too has a projecting wooden gallery with two octagonal dubs on the same side. The building is in bad shape because it has changed hands a number of times, which has led to a lack of maintenance. If restored back to its former glory, it could be used as a guest house as the present owners are willing for any option. The story goes that when the present owners bought the property, they opened the godown to find a priceless collection of Iranian carpets and French crockery. But unfortunately when the carpets were unrolled, they disintegrated into dust!

On the opposite bank that is on your right is a building in direct contrast to the architecture of Hajji Jaffar Khan House. This is Vakil House, where European influence is evident in the combination of circular arches on one floor and near Gothic arches on the floor above.

The Zaina Kadal Bridge that you are standing on right now is a fine example of how bridges were built in Kashmir.

BRIDGES

These bridges are cheap, effective, and picturesque, and their construction ingenious. Old boats filled with stones were sunk at the sites chosen for pier foundation. Piers were then driven and more boats sunk. When a height above the low-water level was reached wooden trestles of deodar were constructed by placing rough-hewn logs at right angles. As the structure approached the requisite elevation to admit of chakwaris (house-boats) passing beneath, the deodar logs were cantilevered. This reduced the span, and huge trees were made to serve as girders to support the roadway. The foundations of loose stones and piles have been protected on the up-stream by planking, and a rough but effective cut-water made. The secret of the stability of these old bridges may perhaps be attributed to the skeleton piers offering little or no resistance to the large volume of water brought down at flood-time. It is true that the heavy floods of 1893 swept away six out of the seven city bridges, and that the cumburous piers tend to narrow the waterway, but it should be remembered that the old bridges had weathered many a serious flood. Not long ago two of the bridges, the Habba Kadal and the Zaina Kadal, had rows of shops on them reminding one of old London, but these have now been cleared away.

Walter R. Lawrence

The Valley of Kashmir

Vakil House, a prosperous merchant's house on the banks of Jhelum river.

After you have crossed this wonderful example of medieval technology turn left along Vakil Street, lined with copper-ware shops, to enter the stone gateway that leads to the tomb of Zain-ul-Abidin's' mother (Budshah's Dumath) and the graveyard of the Sultans.

6 MAZAR-I-SALATEEN

Mazar-i-Salateen is said to have been built on the ruins of a Hindu site dating back to the fourth or fifth century A.D., and consists of the tomb of Sultan Zain-ul-Abidin's mother known as Budshah's Dumath, as well as the royal cemetery known as Mazar-i-Salateen and a public cemetery where many notables of Kashmir lie buried, including a relative of the Mughal Emperor Babur, Mirza Haider Dughlat. This whole complex is enclosed within a massive stone wall, originally with a rigged coping. The entrance to the site is through a trefoliate arched gateway dating back to the Hindu period. A trefoil is a stylized architectural ornament, usually in the form of a three-lobed leaf or flower.

This complex is divided by a broad stone pathway into two parts that culminate at the doorway leading into the walled premises of Mazar-i-Salateen. To the right of the path. along the north eastern corner of the mazar stands the domed tomb Budshah's Dumath. Opposite the tomb, along the north western corner of the mazar, lies the grave of Mirza Haider Dughlat, beneath a mulberry tree. The fore court of the precinct, between the entrance gateway and the walls of the Mazar-i-Salateen, is filled with graves of many prominent Kashmiri poets and nobles. The overall architectural character is a synthesis of Central Asian and Persian influences.

Sultan Zain-ul-Abidin built the tomb for his mother in the fifteenth century. The design of the tomb is

Reusing building materials, particularly stone, from earlier periods is a common architectural practice across the world. So many cathedrals in Mexico rise on the plinths and use the stone masonary of earlier Aztec and Mayan temples. Similarly in India, the first mosque ever to be built, the Quwwat-ul-Islam mosque in Mehrauli (on the outskirts of Delhi), is largely fashioned from pillars taken from Hindu temples that existed earlier in the area. Later rulers such as the Afghans routinely re-used building materials in the Valley, as, for instance. those taken from the Mughal gardens.

said to be modeled on Timur's mausoleum, Gur-i-Amir in Samarkand. The building is the earliest existing brick masonary structure in the region. The design with its central circular dome is a marked departure from the traditional wooden architecture of the region, and shows close affinity with the Persian-Central Asian tomb models.

The entrance is in the form of a horseshoe. The building is a single chamber with a domed ceiling with a height of two storeys. The roof has a central semi-circular dome, and a series of four smaller domes, covered by a decorative brick frieze of blind semi-circular arches. An interesting feature of this building is the use of moulded blue bricks, studded at intervals on the external façade.

The Royal Cemetery is enclosed and contains the cenotaphs of the rulers of the Sultanate. As you enter the domed arched gateway that leads you into the graveyard you will notice two stone sculptures that flank either side of the gateway, probably taken from a Hindu temple. On one of them the defaced figure of a dancing girl is very prominent.

Within the royal cemetery lies the most venerated of all Kashmiri rulers – Budshah Zain-ul-Abidin (for a detailed note on him *see pages* 44–49). His grave is covered by an unassuming plain stone cenotaph apparently a later addition, as the original grave was said to have been covered with a slab of rock crystal. The enclosure is surrounded by a 7-feet-high stone wall decorated with miniature arches and is covered with a sloping stone coping. The area around these cenotaphs has been recently covered with dressed stone paving. In the other part of the cemetery lies the broken grave of Mirza Haider

Mirza Haider Dughlat

Mirza Haider Dughlat was related to Emperor Humayun, who conquered Kashmir in the fifteenth century A.D. He was born at Tashkent, the capital province of Shash, a descendent from the Dughlat tribe, a sub-division of the Chagatay branch of the Mongols. His mother was the sister of Emperor Babur's mother, the founder of the Mughal Empire in India. In 1532 A.D., he conquered Ladakh and then invaded Kashmir. After staying for some time in Kashmir, he was forced to retreat, leaving Kashmir in 1533 A.D. He reconquered it again in 1540 A.D., ruling in the name of Emperor Humayun. His second governership was marked by political and social strife. He is also the author of a famous history detailing the life of the Mughal family entitled *Tarkh-i-Rasheedi*. He was killed in 1551 A.D. in an uprising led by the Chaks and the Magre family and lies buried here.

Dughlat, among others, below a mulberry tree. The three plants that you can see regularly planted at graveyards in Kashmir are the mulberry (toot), the elm (brey) and the celtus australius (brimich). These trees are typically rarely cut or trimmed.

Around the corner from the graveyard is what was once the area inhabited by gold and silversmiths in Srinagar, known as Saraf Kadal. This no longer exists. It was here that the Royal Mint, the Zarab Khana once stood.

As you exit from the Mazar-i-Salateen, turn to your left and walk along the walls of this complex. On your right you will see a five-storied building – a good example of indigenous architecture – with its dub, pinjarakari and dhajji-dewari style of construction. All these terms have been explained in detail in the opening section on Kashmiri architecture.

The royal cemetery, Mazar-i-Salateen, dominated by Zain-ul-Abidin's mother's tomb, Budshah's Dumath.

On your right soon you will come to Kanal Masjid that is located on the first floor above a shop. The building is distinctive because it has mirrors stuck onto its white stucco façade. Just opposite Kanal Masjid is a typical nineteenth-century house with the rastari (basement for storage) and traditional residence above, and its wooden dub.

From this ghat on the opposite bank you can see the Bamzai House where the famous Indian poet-philosopher Rabindranath Tagore was supposed to have stayed when he visited Srinagar in 1915. A small colonial

You may be intrigued by the many sacks of dried unfamiliar plants that you see on the street, outside the traditional spice shops in this area. The extremely long, cold and harsh Kashmir winters necessitate the drying of vegetables through summer and autumn to supplement the mainly rice and meat diet of the winter months. There is sundried cabbage here, goomb which is a dried section of the kadru, dried brinjals and cauliflowers and the distinctive mawal, cockscomb used for colouring. This is also an area where originally fish, both fresh as well as sundried and smokedried used to be sold, but not any longer.

Dried vegetables ready for winter

building on your right is the Maharaja Ganj Primary Health Centre, close to it is the Ramji Mandir with its distinctive shikhara roof. The shikhara comes from the Sanskrit word for mountain peak. Every north Indian temple has a shikhar, an oblong or rectangular tower erected over the main idol in the inner sanctum of the temple.

It is now time to enter the courtyard market, our last stop on this walk that has taken us from khanqah to hammam, the masjid to a cemetery, across bridges and ghats to finally visit a nineteenth century/early twentieth century marketplace.

7 SHRI RANBIR GUNJ SHOPPING COMPLEX

The Maharaja Ranbir Singh (1857–1885) courtyard market is a square collonade of shops around a large central area that was once a courtyard and is now a garden. It was the first planned commercial complex in the city, mostly used by Punjabi (Khatri) retail and wholesale dealers. The complex is based on European patterns, and most of its detailing is derived from the colonial architecture of the region as practiced in the mid-nineteenth and early twentieth century.

The entry to the courtyard is through a series of four openings placed centrally along each of the shopping bays. The building originally had a

At close intervals the river is approached by ruined steps; up and down these the people pass to bathe, to wash their clothes, and to fetch drinking water. The ghats are known as Yarabal, 'the meeting-place of friends'. In the summer, when the vines and other trees are in full leaf, climbing over trellises and falling down the sculptured stones which line the river bank, when the people are splashing about in the water, the highway of the city is a very pretty and lively scene, but its chief beauty is derived from the peeps of the hills and the snow mountains which are caught between the narrow winding alleys running from the river banks.

Walter R. Lawrence
The Valley of Kashmir

---

narrow arched segmental colonnade running along its entire length on both the outer façade as well as along the inner courtyard. The complex still retains many of its original architectural elements including moulded frescos in lime plaster and remnants of decorative pilasters and plaster friezes. The entry to the first floor, presently used mostly as godowns, is located near the corners.

A large part of the colonial charm of the original structure has been lost due to construction that is not in keeping with the building and the purpose it was originally built for. Other sections are in a bad state of repair. With some effort this handsome colonial structure, redolent of the commercial activity of the nineteenth and twentieth century, could be restored to its former glory.

Punjabi traders moved in large numbers into the Valley in 1925, turning Srinagar into even more of a nodal point for the local commercial centres: Baramulla, Islamabad and Sopore. Domestic trade between these centres resulted in tremendous mobility of the population.

Most of these Punjabi traders settled in the city permanently or semi-permanently. In Maharaja Bazaar and Maharaj Gunj, the Punjabi businessmen established their trade monopoly which continued till the advent of militancy in 1989. These bazaars were centres for retail and wholesale business and import-export trade. Salt, sugar, tea, tobacco, snuff, seeds, cotton, metals etc., came to these markets mainly from the Punjab.

1. The Residency
2. Along the Bundh
3. Abe Guzar
4. Along Sheikh Bagh Graveyard
5. The Sadar Court
6. The Lal Chowk Precinct
7. Tyndale Biscoe School
8. The Sher Garhi Complex
9. Gadadar Mandir
10. The Divisional Commissioner Office and the Tehsildar's Office

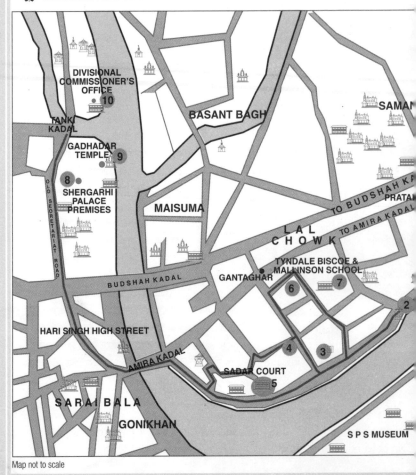

Map not to scale

WALK 2

A Walk Along the Bundh

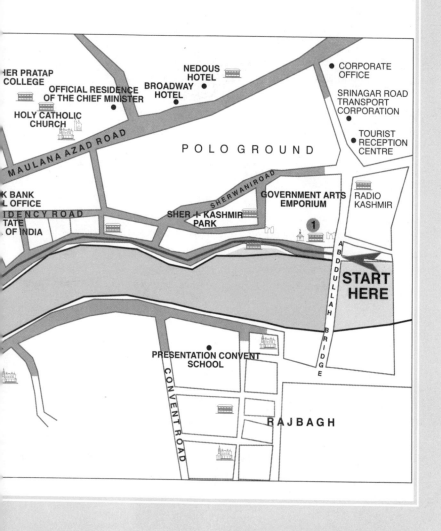

In complete contrast to Walk One is a walk from the Residency, built in the late 1880s, over the bundh where the Britishers would take the air, past the European graveyard of Sheikh Bagh and onto the old court complex: the Saddar Court and one of the oldest schools in Srinagar, the Tyndale Biscoe School. Our walk will culminate at the Sher Garhi Complex. This is a walk where one can relive the history of Srinagar through colonial architecture as many of the buildings are still in use.

THE RESIDENCY

The handsome Residency building, originally constructed around 1885, burnt to the ground in 1998, and was then rebuilt according to the original plan in 2004. A photograph in the hallway as you enter this building shows the original building covered in creepers, possibly ivy. Today this building houses the Jammu and Kashmir Government Handicrafts Emporium.

As you stand on the porch and look across the large garden with its resplendent old chinar and deodar trees (which must date from the time of the building or even earlier) you can look beyond, to the polo ground. The charm of much of the Kashmiri landscape lies in its legacy of old veteran trees – in particular the chinar. These always add to the romantic and timeless character of the place. The avenue of vast chinars planted in straight rows here are in direct contrast to how they are planted in the Mughal gardens of Shalimar and Nishat. Spotting the garden in spring time are spiky jasmine bushes with bright yellow flowers, and magnolia trees. This variety of jasmine is known locally as tehereposh, an allusion to the colour of rice cooked with turmeric, to give it a distinctive bright yellow hue.

In autumn, of course, the flaming yellows, oranges and reds of the chinar

Domination in the colonial town is often expressed in buildings erected by the powers that be. Centres for trade, commerce and administration, cantonments to house the ever increasing army. Till today many public offices are still housed in these European-style buildings: the District Magistrates' headquarters, tax collection office, law courts, police barracks and jail, post and telegraph offices, banks. Hotels, colleges, secondary schools – and, of course, those shops that originally catered exclusively to the colonial customer.

An almost private, secluded world was created by the British in Srinagar where they could 'camouflage their exile through reassuringly familiar surroundings'. It is said of Calcutta at the time that an 'English visitor may come and go almost without realizing that he had been to India at all!'

Western gatehouse to the Residency building.

foliage lend a completely different character to the garden and the Residency Road beyond it. The ground is strewn with the multi-coloured leaves that are collected and later turned into fuel for the Kashmiri's personal heater – the kangri.

On either side of the porch and flight of steps leading up to the entrance, you can see the arched crawl space that allowed for the floodwaters from the Jhelum to swirl around the structure without unduly damaging it. We must remember that the Jhelum flooded often and there was a need to take this into

Deodar

The deodar is widely grown as an ornamental tree, often planted in parks and large gardens and admired for its drooping foliage.

It is among the most cold-tolerant of all trees and originated in the north-west. The curative properties of deodar are well known. The inner wood is aromatic and used to make incense. It is also distilled into essential oil. As insects avoid this tree, the essential oil is used as insect repellant on the feet of horses, cattle and camels. The outer bark and stem are astringent. Deodar's Ayurvedic actions are reported to increase digestive function, remove toxins from the system, alleviate coughing and cure skin disorders such as eczema and psoriasis.

account while designing the Resident's house. The flood of 1893, for instance, was unprecedented as it swept away most of the bridges, damaged houses and submerged the lake gardens, completely decimating the summer diet of melons, cucumbers, tomatoes, and marrows. The government responded to

The first floor of the Residency with its elaborate khatamband ceiling and rows of arches on the verandah that overlooks the Jhelum.

the flood by building high embankments and a large flood canal that would directly drain floodwater from the city into the Wular Lake.

There are two gate houses on your extreme left and right as you face this attractive building, built to impress but not to impose. You can easily imagine carriages entering through the large arches of these gate houses and sweeping up the path to stop at the foot of the steps, women alighting in elegant gowns and gentlemen in their tailcoats and top hats. The Residency gives a real feel of the life of the British in Kashmir.

1885 is a key date in Srinagar's urban history because the accession of the Dogra ruler Maharaja Pratap Singh saw sweeping changes. During his reign the British Residency began in Srinagar with the Resident living in an elegant mansion. The British flag flew over the Residency, all British officers in the state reported directly to him, and he himself actively participated in the state administration.

The western gateway is a rectangular, two-storied structure, while the eastern gateway is a single-storied structure. The main gateway also housed staff members of the Residency, and the British would have had a large and

Kangri

The kangri is an inexpensive and effective heater used to safeguard oneself against the extremely cold winter months. It is a small earthenware pot of a specific quaint shape created by the Krall potters. The pot is held in a designed frame of wicker and cane work, ornamented with wicker rings embellished with bright coloured paper with bunting and beads. The terracotta pot is filled with wood charcoal, dry leaves and live embers and is skillfully carried beneath the pheran or the loi (shawl) of man, woman and child.

The best fuel for the kangri is hak – the small drift-wood collected at the mouth of hill rivers. Dried chinar leaves mixed with cow dung are also commonly used as fuel. Every year in the golden autumn, people sweep dry leaves into heaps, making charcoal for their kangris out of them.

impressive household staff.

A tall gothic arch marks the central gateway, large enough to allow a carriage to pass through. Wooden bands accentuate the horizontal lines of this building. The walls are of burnt brick masonary in lime mortar with horizontal wooden bearing. The windows are pointed arches with extremely decorative wooden frames. However, these gatehouses are in a state of deterioration.

A grand staircase leading to the first floor faces you as you enter the Residency. Within the building, on the right side of the ground floor, is a raised area – perhaps directly copied from the original – which could have been used either as a dance floor or for the placement of a musical band. The three walls within, retained as they were before the fire, indicate that the whole building was constructed with British metric bricks 9 x 4 x 3 inches in size, as opposed to maharaji bricks with which most traditional Kashmiri homes were constructed.

On the first floor, at the rear of the building, a broad verandah overlooks the Jhelum. What is striking here is that the railings and pillars of this verandah, though made of deodar wood are unusually stained a deep brown – known as ambar. This was a dark polish introduced by the British to Kashmir, made of fish glue and copper sulphate combined with either animal, mineral or vegetable dyes to give it a distinctive dark brown colour. Usually, all other woodwork in the Valley is polished a rich russet tone, rogan polish on deodar wood.

ALONG THE BUNDH

It is from the Residency building itself that the bundh (embankment to contain the frequent flooding of the Jhelum) along the river starts. This bundh has recently been refurbished to bring back some of the charm and elegance it

Jammu and Kashmir Bank on Residency Road.

must have had in the late Dogra period.

As you walk along the bundh, the first group of gabled low structures on your right is a set of shops including the famous handicrafts store, Suffering Moses, established in 1840. Next door are the oldest photographers in the Valley, Mahattas, who have a wonderful collection of historic photos of Srinagar, particularly from the pre-independence years.

The next building on your right is what is now Jammu and Kashmir Bank, originally the main office of the travel agency, Cox and Kings. It is a three-storied, linear structure with an attic nestling beneath a steeply pitched roof. The building reminds one of an English country house. The basement (on the side of the Residency Road) is in stone masonary, while the upper two floors are in dhajji-dewari style. The main access to the building faces the bundh and is through a centrally located dhalan (wooden colonnade) leading to the main hall. The building has been renovated on the inside, giving it a totally modern feel.

3 ABE GUZAR

The unusual looking building up ahead on your left, even more striking when you view it from the river or from the opposite bank, is Abe Guzar, the first toll tax post on the river where all boats plying on the Jhelum paid their tax.

The building stands out as a unique example of traditional indigenous architecture, resting on a stone retaining wall. The house is double storied and can also be approached from a gateway opening out onto the River Jhelum.

From an English point of view the valley contains nearly everything which should make life enjoyable. There are sports, varied and excellent, there is scenery for the artist and layman, mountains for the mountaineer, flowers for the botanist, a vast field for the geologist, and magnificent ruins for the archeologist. The epicure will find dainty fruits and vegetables cheaper here than perhaps in any part of the world, while the lounger can pass delightful days of *dolce far ninente* in the mat house-boats moored under the shady chenar tree. And last but not least, the invalid must find somewhere in the varied climate of Kashmir the change of 'air and water' which will restore him to the health of which the heat of the Indian plains have robbed him.

Walter R. Lawrence

The Valley of Kashmir

The gateway is flanked by small circular bastion-like features on either side. Inside there is a single large hall with a high ceiling, opening onto a narrow wooden gallery overlooking the river. The hall is lined with a number of floor to ceiling pointed arched windows with decorative mullion work filled with coloured glass. The gallery is supported on a series of wooden columns that were originally covered with lime plaster. The building, now in a state of neglect, still retains a certain degree of grandeur associated with its past.

Further ahead, on your right, aligned with the new pedestrian bridge across the Jhelum, is the European cemetery of Sheikh Bagh. Sheikh Bagh was named after the only Muslim governor during Sikh rule, who lived here and was also buried here. Europeans camped in this area later, so it seems only appropriate that the Christian graveyard is located here.

All along the banks on your left, particularly between Zero Bridge and the new footbridge at Lal Mandi, you can see a line of boats moored parallel to the recently cleaned banks. Living in a houseboat on the Jhelum is a part of the Kashmiri lifestyle. Early morning and the business of the day begins: washing and drying clothes in the river, preparing food, washing utensils. A small brush of local grasses is used to remove dust from between the wooden floorboards. To clean upholstery, the mattress and cushions are typically just dipped into the river!

On the banks, younger family members are busy in a game of cricket. The Kashmir willow tree fashioned into bats, famous across the world, are in use here, being hit repeatedly with a rubber or plastic ball.

This new footbridge links Lal Mandi and the museum to the bundh on

Abe Guzar, the first toll tax post on the riverfront.

which you are walking, and has put many ferrymen out of business.

4 ALONG SHEIKH BAGH GRAVEYARD

The face we loved is gone
The voice we heard is still
The space left vacant in our hearts,
Never can be filled.

– Epitaph on a gravestone

Stepping into the graveyard is like stepping into the past. Huge brooding chinars stand tall. Overgrown foliage, scattered flowers, low creepers surround the old graves. Here is a fallen gravestone overgrown with moss, there, an elegant elongated statue of a young woman who died in the prime of life. Time stands still here. Even though many of the graves lie unkempt and

overgrown – the epitaphs on the gravestones tell the story of another age.

One died climbing a mountain, another was a famous golfer, the third the butler of a British family. You can spend an interesting hour here reading the gravestones, and looking at the statuary that conjures up the past. Images float up – ladies taking the air on the bundh next door, beggars lining the street to the graveyard in its heyday, visits by descendents of those buried here. Quiet, unkempt, this cemetery is a record of a silent historical presence. Outside the high walls time has moved on – buses, traffic, soldiers alert on duty – the serenity of the graveyard lies unruffled within its tall walls.

You must walk through one of the small alleys on your right to make your way to the Saddar Court on the other side. These contain good examples of Kashmiri indigenous architecture with its distinctive dubs, deedhs, and pinjarakari.

We are now in what was the nerve centre of Srinagar in Dogra times, and the overriding influence of the British ruling by proxy can be seen. Western style buildings created an environment in which Indians were exposed to European ideas of education, justice, administration, even the post and telegraph system! An Indian student studying the classics including Shakespeare attended classes in Western style buildings (like the Tyndale Biscoe School), received medical treatment in a western hospital, mailed a letter from a post office and testified in the Sadar Court. Colonialism often expressed itself most completely in architectural terms, and the strong influence a British 'environment' had on the Indian mind is obvious.

THE SADAR COURT

Originally known as the Sadar Court in which the Ranbir Singh Penal Code was levied out, this building is now known as the Court of the Additional and District Judge. It is a fine and striking example of colonial architecture.

The main entrance to the building is through a three-storied stone porch having arched openings on the northern side, leading into the main hall. The building façade is dominated by a linear wooden balcony projecting out from the first floor to the right of the main porch. Most of the window openings of the building are segmental or circular with rectangular wooden

Beautiful gravestone of a Britisher in the Sheikh Bagh graveyard.

window frames. The second floor is in brick masonary with lime mortar.

6 THE LAL CHOWK PRECINCT

The Lal Chowk precinct which stretches on both sides of the Amira Kadal–Biscoe road has remained as the main business centre of Srinagar from the early twentieth century. The area developed as a continuous linear extension of the commercialized areas of Hari Singh High Street and Maharaji Bazaar.

Some of the earlier buildings here include the Gandha Singh building, which burnt down, Sahani Lodge, the Baghat building and the Gurudwara. Most of these were built in the last decades of the nineteenth century or in the opening years of the twentieth century. Many of them still retain their original colonial features. Some major establishments here included the Palladium Cinema (burnt down in 1990s), the Lalla Rukh Hotel and the Tyndale Biscoe School. It was here that Sheikh Abdullah and India's first Prime Minister Jawaharlal Nehru had their first public gathering. During 1980s, a clock tower known as Ghanta Ghar was constructed at the centre of the precinct. Many portions of the precinct have been rebuilt, diluting the colonial charm and original architectural cohesion of this precinct.

The road leading from the Sadar Court to the Amira Kadal Bridge is narrow and lined with mostly colonial style buildings, including the Gurudwara. Some of the building façades are dominated by segmental arched arcades or long wooden galleries. From the Court Road uptill the Biscoe School, the precinct opens out in the form of a U-shaped place lined with both modern and colonial buildings. These are mainly three- or four-stories tall. A large parking space has recently been created by the Srinagar Municipal Corporation in the centre of this plaza.

❼ TYNDALE BISCOE SCHOOL

Within the Tyndale Biscoe School complex is a building reminiscent of an English country house and that was possibly modeled on a rural English cottage. The building comprises a two-storied, linear building with an attic floor beneath a steeply pitched roof. The main façade which is constructed in the traditional dhajji-dewari style, is dominated by a series of bays, dormers, and gables making the building very picturesque.

❽ THE SHER GARHI COMPLEX

The Sher Garhi complex came into being while the Afghans were ruling Kashmir (1752-1819) through their governors. Other than building the fortifications that crown the Hari Parbhat Hill, they chose to move the residence of the governor several kilometers south, to a bend in the Jhelum River, now known as Sher Garhi.

Of all the Afghan rulers of Kashmir the most benign was Amir Khan Jawan Sher (1770–1777) who constructed the original Sher Garhi Palace and the Amira Kadal Bridge, but also destroyed some of the Mughal Gardens on the Dal Lake. While the palace of both Yousuf Chak and of the Afghan governor have long since disappeared or burnt down, in their place we have the Dogra palace.

Architecture in the hundred and one years of Dogra rule (1846–1947) clearly reflected the changes in styles and norms of colonial and imperial architecture in other parts of India. The use of porches, gables, turrets, gothic windows, frontages with verandahs and galleries, the overall volume and feel, as well as decorative features – particularly in wood, brick, stucco, and stone marked this period of architecture. A number of different structures built over the Dogra years in the Sher Garhi Complex are good examples of these.

The actual durbar (assembly) hall of the original palace is a two-storied imposing building with a curved frontage – unusual by itself in Kashmiri architecture. The façade is marked by two tall Corinthian columns with carved

Canon Tyndale Biscoe, who arrived in Srinagar in 1890, took over as headmaster of the Mission School that had been established by the Reverend Doxey in 1882. He remained in Kashmir for fifty years and made himself famous by sending the boys onto the streets to put out fires, which occurred regularly. He also insisted that the boys learn to swim, which had earlier been considered improper, so that they could help save lives during the frequent flooding of the Jhelum. What the boys who were mainly the sons of the influential, Kashmir Pandits needed, Biscoe believed was 'not brain training but heart changing.'

> The picturesque palace which stands next to the golden temple was built by Maharaja Ranbir Singh, and is a reminiscence of the Dogra country. New palaces of another style are springing up, and before long the Sher Garhi will be a mass of large buildings. Across the river is the finest ghat in Srinagar, the Basant Bagh, with grand stone steps pillaged from the mosque of Hassanabad. In the old days a rope was stretched from Basant Bagh to the palace and petitions were hauled up from the river to Maharaja Gulab Singh's hall of audience.
>
> **Walter R Lawrence**
> *The Valley of Kashmir*

capitals, lending an air of grandeur and ceremony to the structure. The symmetrical building plan and grand dog-legged staircase leading out of a central foyer are other distinctive features of colonial architecture here. This palace till recently served as the Jammu and Kashmir Legislative Assembly and therefore, for security reasons, is closed to visitors.

However, a brief description of the other buildings in this complex follows, and it is certainly worth visiting this complex and the adjoining one, now housing the Divisional Commissioner's Office, to get a flavour of official and palace life in the Dogra period. Do keep in mind, however, that all of these buildings are still in use as government offices, which means while they are open to the public, they are also crowded and busy.

What can be visited is the building that houses the Department of Archives, Archaeology and Museums, the large building of stone masonary on the ground floor and brick masonary on the other two floors.

This building can easily be approached from Shaheed Gunj. A magnificent example of colonial architecture during Dogra rule, its frontage has three projecting bays. The building is 50 x 150 feet and is approximately 30 feet high. While the ground floor has cement flooring, the other storeys have wooden floors.

In the courtyard between the palace and the Archives building stands a small stone pavilion. It faces a large wooden door with two bay windows, above which was the entrance that used to lead from the Palace to the Administrative Block. This elegant pavilion is made up of open archways below a dome, with four cupolas at the corners of the dome. The pavilion is built in devri stone, and the pillars have curved bases with flowers on their capitals.

You could also walk around the building that faces it, with the boards of the Directorate of Local Bodies and Khadi Board clearly displayed, to see what is known as Block D, a wonderful example of colonial architecture. Next to both of these is a temple, the Gadadar Temple, and its forecourt looks over the river.

Block D, now completely abandoned, is a four-storied building facing the river. What is unique here are the cast iron pillars and balcony painted bright blue, offsetting the cream and green walls. The large fissures on the walls are, however, an indication that this property is condemned and will soon be brought down.

 GADADAR MANDIR

From the terrace that forms the forecourt to the Gadadar temple you can get an idea of the spatial orientation of the entire complex and how it relates to the surrounding geography. Directly opposite the steps or ghat leading down to the river, is the Basant Bagh Ghat. It was here, in what was once an orchard, petitioners waited their turn to cross the river and deliver their petitions to the court. There was a chabutra on this ghat which acted as a resting place for the petitioners. A huge bell was hung over the chabutra, suspended from a chinar tree. This was rung to call the petitioners. On the right of the Basant Bagh Ghat you can see the Tsunt Canal (Apple Canal) that is a direct link to the Dal Lake.

> The shikhara is a key element in the design of any temple. It comes from the Sanskrit word shikhar meaning mountain peak, and refers to the oblong shaped tower above the sanctum of the temple.

Up the river, on your extreme right, though you can't see it, is the Budshah Bridge. On your left is the District Commissoner's office (what was once Amar Singh's residence) on the other side of a moat built by Yousuf Chak. And yes, up ahead on your left, glinting in the sunshine are the fortifications of Hari Parbhat.

Gadadar Mandir, a temple constructed for the use of the royal family of the Maharaja is situated within the palace premises. The Maharaja would worship in the temple daily before going to the durbar. The temple is rectangular in plan with the inner sanctum located off centre. The entrance to the temple is aligned along the east-west axis. There is another entrance from the river which has a separate ghat. The shikhara of the temple is dome shaped, topped with a finial and is gold plated.

The exterior of the Secretariat Complex previously known as Sher Garhi.

Walk out of this complex and turn into the next gate on your right that now houses the Divisional Commissioner's Office, but was once the residence of Amar Singh, father to Hari Singh, the last Dogra ruler of Kashmir.

🪷 THE DIVISIONAL COMMISSIONER OFFICE AND THE TEHSILDAR'S OFFICE

Facing the river and built in dhajji-dewari style, this two-storied structure is a handsome building. Turned pillars in dark wood surround the gabled porch of this building now painted white. Built on a stone plinth, the corners of the building and details above the arches are really of brick, not stone, painted to resemble quoin.

The entire building has plenty of decorative features; the ornate brackets supporting the projections, the glass work in the windows, carved eaves, the ceiling of skillfully crafted khatambandh, displaying unusual patterns in different rooms. Two turrets with gothic windows mark the extreme corners of this building.

A khatambandh ceiling on the porch and an elaborately carved wooden square doorway leads into the main foyer with a rectangular wooden staircase leading to the upper floors. This staircase is highlighted by ornate banisters and big newel posts. The first floor has other administrative offices and a large conference hall with richly carved doors. An interesting feature of this hall are the glazed partition sliding doors which have cut glass pieces joined with lead in geometric patterns and Belgian crystal door bars. Almost all the rooms have fireplaces and carved wooden dado work.

> Quoin is an architectural feature in which the corners of a building are, or give the appearance of being solid, to distinguish it from the rest of the building surface.

This bungalow was once connected to the Shergarhi Palace by a bridge. Later the building also served as offices of the Wazir-i-Wazarat. However, after 1947 this post was abolished, and it has been used as the office of the Divisional Commissioner since then.

Walk around this building and to your right you see the Tehsildar's Office, another striking example of colonial architecture. The open plan staircase that faces you is a recent addition, but the traditional layout of the building has its own charm with open verandahs on each floor leading into the rooms. The blank arches that decorate the façade are typical of this period of architecture.

Today's walk has taken us in a sweep along the riverfront from the Residency to the Sher Garhi Complex, symbols of the ruling power of the colonialists and the Dogras. You have visited a spectrum of buildings, constructed between 1880 and the 1930s, that demonstrate the variety of form and function in colonial architecture.

1 Shalimar Gardens
2 Nishat Gardens
3 Pari Mahal

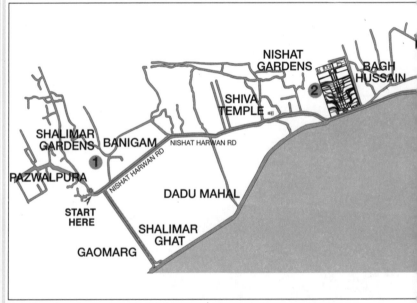

Map not to scale

WALK 3

A Garland of Gardens

Apple blossoms

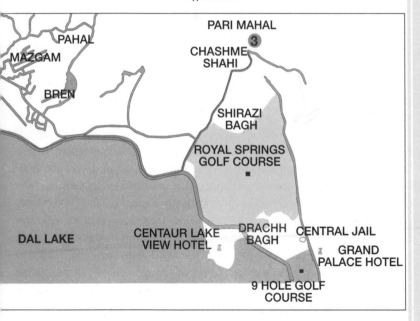

PARI MAHAL

PAHAL

MAZGAM

CHASHME
SHAHI

BREN

SHIRAZI
BAGH

ROYAL SPRINGS
GOLF COURSE

DRACHH
BAGH

CENTRAL JAIL

DAL LAKE

CENTAUR LAKE
VIEW HOTEL

GRAND
PALACE HOTEL

9 HOLE GOLF
COURSE

Today's walk-cum-drive will take you in a sweep on Boulevard Road around the grand old Dal Lake. You can begin by spending time in what was once the most famous garden in the world, Shalimar Gardens, designed by Emperor Jahangir and his son, Shah Jahan. Then, onto Nishat Gardens – a delight at any time of the year – built over three centuries ago by the Empress Noor Jahan's brother, Asaf Khan. Finally, a 20-minute drive will take you to Pari Mahal, created by Asaf Khan's grandson and great Sufi believer, Prince Dara Shikoh. (For more on the Mughals *see pages* 52-61).

THE MUGHAL GARDENS

The enclosed garden is a Persian concept, and is often described as being similar to the garden of paradise. Paradise is seen in Islamic religious scriptures as being a garden with streams. Unlike the rigid formality of French and English gardens with their elaborate layout based on geometry and hedges cut into box-like shapes, a spirit of harmony between the natural and the manmade pervades the Mughal gardens.

The Persian garden is typically a charbagh, four gardens divided by four channels of water (symbolizing the four rivers of life) flanked by paved causeways. It was this concept that the Mughals brought to the Valley, building as many as seventy-seven gardens during their reign of over 150 years. Flower beds, flowering bushes and fruit trees coupled with fountains and waterways were offset by delicate pavilions in each of the gardens they built. Water was a major element of the design, both still and in motion, and it was important not only to see it, but also to hear it. Water also played a major function – it irrigated and cooled the garden.

Compared to the gardens of Agra and Delhi, the undulating landscape of Kashmir and the endless supply of water from running mountain streams introduced two new dimensions into the formal Mughal garden of the hills. Pools of still water were replaced by cascades and flowing channels, and the gardens and pavilions were located on gradually ascending levels. Otherwise, the layout remained the same as in the plains. There were flagged walkways dividing flat rectangular garden areas carved out of the foothills into formal square spaces with trees and flower beds planted in lines along the channeled paths of flowing water. At strategic points of change of level, elegant stone pavilions were erected. Entry to such a garden was typically through a gatehouse located on the garden's main axis.

Facing page: The formal geometric charbagh layout of the Shalimar Gardens, with water causeways, fountains, paths, and pavilions.

1 SHALIMAR GARDENS

As with all the other Mughal gardens of Kashmir, Shalimar Bagh was primarily an encampment site for the visiting Mughal emperor and his vast entourage. While it was Emperor Jahangir who conceptualized the layout of this garden, his son Shah Jahan collaborated with him in its design, while he was still a prince.

Shalimar is arranged in a series of five terraces rising one above the other, all of nearly equal dimensions. A line of tanks is placed symmetrically down the middle of these terraces and these are connected by a nehar (canal), 18 feet deep and about 9 to 14 yards wide. The edge of each of the five terraces has something interesting to offer either in the form of a baradari, a water pool with playing fountains, or a rushing cascade.

The water comes from a branch of the Arrah spring that is also the principal feeder to the Dal Lake. It enters at the upper end, flows through each successive terrace in beautiful stone chutes, carved in many ingenious patterns of shell and fish, leading to the reservoir below that contains numerous fountains, and, after leaving the garden, falls into the outer canal that leads to the lake. These tanks and canals with fountains and cascades were originally lined with polished limestone, resembling black marble.

Shalimar was originally divided into three main areas: an outer or public garden on the lowest three terraces, which contain the grand canal leading from the lake and ending with the first large pavilion. This is the Diwan-i-Aam (where the emperor held public audience), which contains a small black marble throne. The upper two levels were exclusively for the emperor and his courtiers and hence were called the Diwan-i-Khas.

These two parts were screened from each other by means of a thick masonary wall having two similar gateways at each side of the water channel. The dividing wall between the Diwan-i-Aam and Diwan-i-Khas was dismantled early in the 1980s for the popular Son et Lumiere shows. So there is no longer·a clear demarcation between these two royal zones. A ruined hammam is located in the middle of these two terraces and also embedded within the boundary wall.

And finally there is the zenana garden for the women of the harem, containing a large black marble pavilion and elaborate waterworks set in a cross around it. A traditional charbagh, the zenana garden was the crowning glory of the Shalimar and, when its many fountains and watery arcades were lit up at night with lanterns, the spectacle would have been overwhelming.

This pavilion on the fourth level is raised upon a platform, a little more than 3 feet high and 65 feet square. Its sloping roof is about 20 feet high and is supported, on each side, by a row of six elaborately carved black marble pillars,

A cascade of water runs through a pavilion in the Shalimar Garden built by Mughal Emperor Shah Jahan.

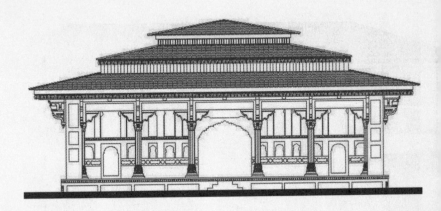

Elevation of pavilions in the Shalimar Gardens.

which are flitted and polygonal in shape. It was used as a banqueting hall, a favourite place for various kinds of entertainment. The pavilion is surrounded by a reservoir; 52 yards square and about 3.5 inches deep. It is lined with stone and contains a hundred-and-forty large fountains.

Upon each side of the terrace, built against the wall, there is also a lodge. These formed the private dwellings of the royal family.

On the edge of each of the three lower terraces a small pavilion overlooks the fountains in the tank below. Each pavilion consists of two apartments on the side of the canal, over which is a covered archway uniting the two, and that of the lowest is supported by 16 black stone pillars which are fluted and polygonal in shape.

The Mongols, who were the Mughal's ancestors, had always pitched their tents in gardens such as these, and often held their courts here. Over time just as the palace tent got translated into stone, so did the tent in the garden become the permanent roofed pavilion. Under Noor Jahan the garden was no longer just a place of private pleasure, it now hosted imperial functions, providing the public and also other higher petitioners, official access to the emperor.

Even today you can find large Kashmiri families picnicking in the garden with their samovar and wicker baskets, following a custom of the nineteenth century when day-long picnics were organized in these gardens to escape the crowded streets of the old city.

2 NISHAT GARDENS

In 1626, Asaf Khan, the wily only brother of the Empress Noor Jehan, built the magnificent Nishat Gardens. He belonged to one of the first families of Mughal India. Originally from Persia, this family played a formidable role in Mughal

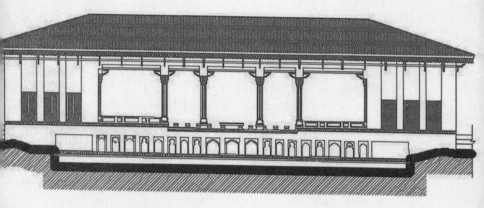

politics; his father Itmad-ul-Daulah was the vizier of Jahangir, while his sister Noor Jehan married the Emperor Jahangir. Asaf Khan himself was vizier and father-in-law to Emperor Shah Jahan, as his daughter Mumtaz Mahal married Shah Jahan.

In Central Asia, gardens were often built on gentle slopes that lent themselves to terraced gardens. The Mughals sought to recreate this in Kashmir around the Dal Lake. The Nishat Gardens unfolds in a series of eleven steps down the mountainside overlooking the Dal Lake. There were originally 12 steps – but now the lowest has become the actual road itself. It is said that the original twelve steps or terraces (tabakat) represented the 12 signs of the zodiac.

Visit the steps of the Nishat in early spring to see the luxuriant white and pink blossoms of almond, plum, and peach. 'As the snow melts, their whiteness is rivaled by the delicate sprays of early fruit blossoms as seen across the dark background of the cypress trees; while the pink mist of almond and apricot flowers in little patches of colour against the bare hill-sides. Soon the ground under the trees is carpeted with bulbs, scillas, tulips, hyacinth, fritillaries and iris … . Lilac, jasmine and carnations follow; then last and best of all come the roses. This could certainly be a description of any of the Mughal Gardens in spring, but actually this is a description of gardens elsewhere.'

But, certainly the most imposing of all trees here are the magnificent huge chinars. The Kashmir Valley and the chinar are synonymous. Almost every village in the Valley has one chinar tree, if not more. Some even have groves that date back a few hundred years!

On the top step of the Nishat Gardens stands a shingled roof pavilion, based on the design of a typical Mughal structure, not unlike the roofed pavilions in the Shalimar gardens. Rebuilt during the reign of Maharaja Ranjit Singh, the building

Residents of Srinagar enjoy a lively chat sitting in one of the pavilions in the Nishat Gardens.

incorporates some original features linked to the Mughal period, such as the stonework of the chadder and the stone bases of the wooden column. It consists of a central rectangular open pavilion with a room on either side on the first floor. Both the side rooms are almost square in shape, with a single floor-length window located on the main western façade. A small, low, centrally located door provides access to the pavilion from the room. The ground floor is filled with earth and has no access.

The pavilion is based on the pattern of a traditional dalan with a water channel passing through the centre, cascading down the stone chadder into a pool located at the ground floor level. The main façade is dominated by a series of alcoves detailed as blind cusped arches. The ceiling of the pavilion is supported by four-fluted (twelve-sided) wooden columns. A traditional Kashmiri style chaar baam roof, covered with wooden shingles surmounts the building. The shingles on the roof are made of deodar wood, the mainstay of all Kashmir architecture. Deodar shingles are effective because they are moisture-resistant and also impervious to rain. Of course, as with anything else made of wood, they need regular maintenance.

The retaining wall on the last terrace of the garden stretches between two octagonal towers (burj). The towers, located on the northern and southern corners, have been partially restored over a period of time. The ground floors of both these towers consist of an octagonal chamber covered with shallow brick

THE FLOWERS OF THE VALLEY

'The flowers of Kashmir are beyond counting or calculation. What shall I write of? How many can I describe?' wrote Emperor Jahangir in his memoirs.

With its several changes of season, the Kashmiri landscape completely transforms itself from a mantle of snow to a profusion of flowers to a russet autumn every year.

Early in March the gardens begin to wake from a long winter sleep, and although the grass is brown and the trees are leafless many a garden is found filled with masses of violets, pansies, wall flowers, narcissi, crocuses, and daisies. Willow buds show signs of bursting open and the apricot trees are almost ready to blossom. By the beginning of April the English primroses which were introduced by Sir Francis Younghusband are in full bloom, together with daffodils and hyacinths, while the apricot and peach trees form little clouds of delicate pink and white blossoms.

Tulips and irises are blooming by the middle of April, closely followed by poppies and peonies. By the first of May the rambler roses are out and by the middle of the month the strawberries are ripe. By the end of the month the gardens are glorious with geraniums, delphiniums, poppies and sweet peas. June brings the gladioli. Canterbury bells, pink carnations, sweet willams and foxgloves and by the end of the month the fuchsias and hollyhocks are at the height of their glory.

When the spring flowers are all gone, we see in their places the tufted spikes of the rich red ploygonum, the tall lavender like stachys, the dwarf mauve swertia land delphiniums with large bowl-shaped flowers. Above the forest the slopes are clothed with miles of junipes bush in dense dark green patches among which red, orange and yellow clumps of euphorbia with oleander like leaves form beautiful masses of colour.

In September, asters, zinnia, salvia, cannas, fuchsias, and geraniums are at the height of their beauty followed a month later by row after row of flaming chinar, the ground thickly blanketed by orange and red fallen leaves. The sun then loses its strength and by December/January the whole valley wears a thick mantle of snow once again.

Walter R. Lawrence
The Valley of Kashmir

masonary domes. The outer façade of the building is flanked by a series of six-arched arcades, with one of the arcades facing the terrace, containing a door opening on the ground floor. The rooms have two low and centrally located doors and are covered by a vaulted ceiling. A narrow, steep staircase, located within the wall provides access to the upper floors.

Though Nishat, like most other Islamic gardens is set within a boundary wall, yet this does not isolate the garden from its surroundings. In the traditional char bagh one finds the boundary wall acting as a barrier to protect the self-created 'paradise' from the harsher environment surrounding it. But in the case of Nishat, the only purpose of the wall is security and its impact on the garden and its surroundings are negligible. The continuity of view as the eye travels from the Dal Lake to the Zabarwan Mountain remains intact.

It is the harmony and continuity of this relation between the garden and the landscape that surrounds it, that sets Nishat apart from the rest of the Mughal gardens in Kashmir, making it the most exquisite example of a 'Garden of Paradise.'

Among the other trees here are magnolias, cypress and chestnuts, yellow jasmine bushes with their vivid star like flowers, iris (known locally as mazhaar munj, the bulb of the graveyard) narcissus, flocks, and poppies. These are all being planted at the present, with some beginning to bloom. Foliage in the Nishat includes several trees, shrubs and flowers well represented in Persian poetry: the chinar and cypress, daffodils and hyacinth, narcissus and rose.

Down the centre of the steps of the Nishat Garden runs a water channel – which drops from one level to the other over artificially built waterfalls. In some places there are fountains (at the present water is pumped up into these) but originally these were made of klubes terracotta (baked clay) pipes which pushed water up into low fountains that functioned according to gravity. As in all Mughal gardens these fountains were of low intensity – water spilling constantly out of fountainheads to create the restful sound of flowing water.

The waterfalls – created of textured stone – are cut in different shapes to create different sounds. They are a clear indication of the fine attention to detail. Each level therefore has a variation in the sound of water!

The water channel is bridged over by a number of rectangular and octagonal stone thrones (platforms or bridges) at various levels. These stone thrones provide some of the best viewing points of the garden and are supposed to be of the Mughal period. The octagonal thrones located on the ninth and tenth terrace are decorated with beautiful motifs.

An associated feature of the water channel is the presence of pools or talabs in the vicinity of each cascade. There are four large and a series of small pools within the garden. On starry nights the pools must have served as ideal backdrops for night time performances with the light of oil lamps (diyas) flickering in the air behind sheets of water cascading from above.

In the immediate vicinity of the Shalimar and Nishat Gardens is the site of Harwan from where many of the beautiful terracotta tiles were recovered, and are now on display at the Pratap Singh Museum. A fifteen-minute drive up the mountains, past another garden, the Chashme Shahi, brings you to Pari Mahal.

❸ PARI MAHAL

Under the peaks of the Zabarwan mountains perched on a spur, stands the pale cream and beige masonary structure of the Pari Mahal (the Palace of the Fairies) and, on a clear morning, afternoon or even evening, when the clouds have gone – this site is celestial. Look down from a height of approximately 600 feet to the majesty of the Dal Lake, the Royal Springs (yes, Chashme Shahi) Golf Course in the foreground. From this height, the Dal appears as though made of molten metal, and the entire valley often seems wrapped in mist. Marooned in the middle of the lake is the tiny Char Chinar Island, dwarfed by the vast, still waters of the lake.

The stepped garden of Pari Mahal is full of huge purple and yellow poppies, foxgloves in pink and yellow, peach and white – cut cypress trees in symmetrical rows and magnolia trees with their waxy leaves whose foliage is at its peak in early summer.

On the topmost terraces are the ruins of a baradari overlooking the lake and a reservoir built against the mountainside. At each corner of this terrace steps lead down to the next level where you can find an arched wall, with 21 arches built in descending order from the centre. The third level has the entrance to the garden through a domed chamber. Some of the walls in this building are said to have contained earthen pipes.

You can just imagine the Mughal Crown Prince Dara Shikoh in these environs, walking through the rough limestone block and masonary arches which were perhaps dressed at that time in stucco. It was here on this mountain that time could be spent in silent meditation, far from the din of the medieval encampment of over a lakh of retainers, and the distant fort on Hari Parbat – almost Japanese in shape – as far as far can be. Communication with the fort and other gardens from this lovely spot were through the use of pigeons and the pigeon house is the largest structure in the complex, located on the fifth level.

1. Kathi Darwaza
2. The Mullah Shah Mosque
3. The Hammam of Dara Shikoh
4. Badaamwari

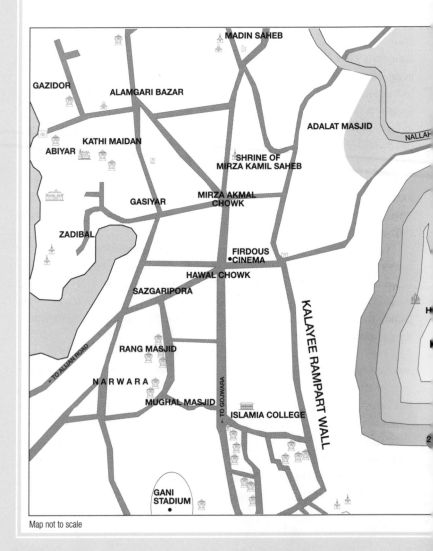

Map not to scale

WALK 4

Exploring Hari Parbat

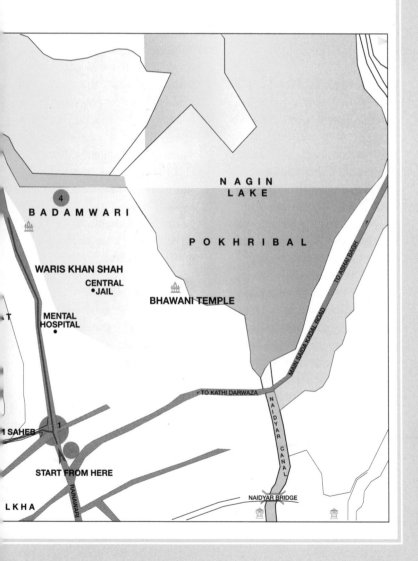

Today we travel up Hari Parbhat where the Mullah Shah complex celebrates a Sufi master, who found royal patronage from the eldest son and daughter of the Mughal Emperor Shah Jahan, Dara Shikoh and Jehanara Begum. Here we will visit a mosque, a caravanserai and a hammam. We end today's walk in the beautiful almond garden or Badaamwari on the same hill that has been recently constructed on the site of a garden that existed in the Afghan period.

The hill that dominates the Srinagar skyline, Hari Parbat has a spectrum of different structures built over the centuries. At the absolute top is the actual fortification built by the Afghans in 1810-1815, no longer accessible to the public. This fort was built by Atta Mohammed Khan, the governor of Kashmir, who renounced the authority of his superiors in Kabul. The fort was completed by his successor Mohammed Azim Khan (1813-19). Prominent architectural structures on this hill include the recently developed landscape garden: the Badaamwari, the shrine of Makhdoom Sahib and just below it, the Mullah Shah complex.

How Hari Parbat came into being

According to legend the Kashmir Valley was once a vast lake called Satisar, the 'lake of sati' named after Parvati. Parvati's permanent abode was on the shore of Satisar in the foothills of mount Haramoukh. Despite her divine presence demons headed by Jalodbhava ('water-born'), came to infest the lake. They killed and devoured human beings who lived on the shores of the lake. In desperation, the people appealed to Kashyapa — the grandson of the god Brahma — to save them from Jalodbhava and his horde.

Kashyapa offered penance for one thousand years to rid the people of the demons. His prayers were finally granted. Goddess Sharika appeared before him in the form of a hari (Kashmiri word for the myna bird), with a pebble in her beak. This she deftly dropped over the demon, Jalodbhava. The pebble grew bigger and bigger, assuming the form of a hillock, that submerged the demon Jalodbhava, hence, the name of the hillock, Hari Parbat. With the monsters out of the way Kashyapa drained the lake at a depression in the Valley near Baramulla, and the Valley was named after him. Kashgapa-Mar which became Kashmir over time.

1 KATHI DARWAZA

Historical records show that Prince Dara Shikoh constructed a palace in the foothills of the Koh-i-Maran hillock. The palace was built within the walled Mughal city of Nagar Nagar that had been founded by Emperor Akbar. He had this built as a response to the terrible famine of 1597 that coincided with his last visit to the Valley. Akbar's response to the famine was to provide employment, and he had a fortification built around the imperial forces stationed at Hari Parbhat. Today, other than the stone rampart wall

The Mullah Shah Mosque on the way to the Makhdoom Sahib shrine.

and the two entrance gateways (Sangeen Darwaza and Kathi Darwaza), not much remains of this Mughal endeavour.

Subsequently a number of Mughal kings, princes and governors embellished the city of Nagar Nagar with palaces, ateliers, and gardens. None of these buildings have survived. Of the palace constructed by Dara Shikoh the only surviving remnant is a hauz or well, now filled with garbage. Isolated masonary remnants are scattered across the area, that suggest a variety of different structures once stood here.

It was to the west of his palace, on a slightly elevated piece of land, that Dara Shikoh constructed a mosque for his mentor, Mullah Shah, known as the Mullah Shah Masjid.

2 THE MULLAH SHAH MOSQUE

As you ascend the steps leading to the Makhdoom Sahib shrine, the Mullah Shah complex is on your left. When you enter the courtyard, the actual mosque is to your right. Immediately in front of you and at a lower level, is what was once a garden with a pavilion, while on your left are the ruins of a caravanserai and even further, in the extreme left corner, the recently rebuilt hammam.

Mullah Shah

Mullah Shah was born in 1584 A.D, in the village of Erkesa in Badakshan. At the age of 22 he left home and travelled, finally finding his spiritual mentor, Mian Mir.

Mian Mir was the leading Sufi saint of the seventeenth century belonging to the Qadari order, with his khanqah at Lahore. The heat of Lahore did not suit Mullah Shah so he decided to spend the summers in Kashmir, returning to Lahore to attend upon Mian Mir in winter. In 1636 A.D. he returned, as usual, to Lahore from Kashmir, and practiced his austerities until one day he attained what is referred to in Sufi terminology as Union with God. In Kashmir, Mullah Shah collected around him a small circle of disciples, which over time included believers drawn from various social classes, even women.

But the orthodox Muslims, affronted by his views, sent a petition to the Mughal Emperor Shah Jahan, requesting him to sentence Mullah Shah to death. The emperor consented, and dispatched a firman (royal order) to Zafar Khan, the governor of Kashmir. Mullah Shah was saved from certain death by the intervention of Shah Jahan's eldest son, Prince Dara Shikoh. Meanwhile Mullah Shah had become so fond of solitude that he rarely showed himself in the city of Srinagar. In 1639, Emperor Shah Jahan, on a visit to Kashmir, sent for Mullah Shah. He received him kindly and they conversed for a long time on subjects relating to Sufism. It was during this visit of the Mughal royal family that Dara Shikoh met Mullah Shah for the very first time, and became his disciple. Like his grandfather Emperor Akbar, Prince Dara Shikoh was fascinated by the similarity between different religions, and was in many ways what we now call a 'secularist'. The eldest sister of Dara, Jehanara Begum, also became a member of the exclusive circle surrounding the Sufi saint. Mullah Shah developed great affection for the princess and used to remark, 'she has attained such an extraordinary degree of knowledge that she is fit to be my successor.'It is said that the three of them: Mullah Shah, Dara Shikoh and Jehanara Begum established a carpentry and masonary workshop here on the hill of Hari Parbat. After the execution of Dara Shikoh and Aurangzeb's accession to the Mughal throne, there was an attempt to instigate the new emperor against Mullah Shah, but fortunately Jehanara Begum intervened. Subsequently Aurangzeb invited the Mullah to visit him at Lahore. It was not till 1660 A.D. that Mullah Shah could comply, and, leaving Srinagar at the beginning of winter, he came to Lahore, where he continued to live a retired life, only meeting with a few chosen disciples. After his death in 1661, Jehanara Beghum erected a shrine of red sandstone over his grave in Lahore.

The mosque of Mullah Shah is unique in that it comprises a quadrangle or courtyard mosque within a surrounding quandrangle. The outer quadrangle consists of the main entrance gateway and a series of cells on the north, with an extension on the western side. The cells (hujra or khilwatgah) are said to have been used by members of Mullah Shah's entourage for solitary worship. Another possible interpretation is that these rooms served as residences for the masons in Mullah Shah's workshop. Facing you is the eastern façade of the

> The proportions of this building (Mullah Shah Mosque), the simplicity
> of its surface treatment, its architectural character and manipulation
> generally, are all most commendable. Particularly noticeable are the
> archways whether plain, pointed or engrailed, as they are singularly
> graceful in their curves, while the scheme of the back wall exterior,
> with a projection to mark the recessed mihrab in the interior is well
> conceived. In many respects this ruined neglected structure is a model
> in miniature of an appropriate mosque composition.
> **Percy Brown**
> *Indian Architecture: The Islamic Period*

mosque across a spacious lawn with three mature chinar trees. A square depression in the middle of the open area suggests the possible location of the ablution tank or hauz. Further to the east, a staircase leads to rooms at the lower level that form the caravanserai.

The mosque is built of a masonary core clad with fine dressed limestone. On certain façades delicate Arabic calligraphy from the Quran can be seen. The entrance portal is decorated with a beautiful stone guldista. An intricate floral stone frieze marks the plinth on the outer façade. A number of small holes are punched into the decorative designs of the mosque walls within the courtyard, but their function is yet to be understood.

The mosque consists of four linear halls or iwans surrounding a small paved courtyard approximately 30 x 30 feet. The eastern hall is the main prayer hall with the mehrab and minber opening out onto the courtyard through a second portal, in turn surmounted by the main dome of the building. The upper floor of the mosque comprises a low height gallery looking onto the courtyard below. The height of this gallery makes it impossible for it to be used for prayer.

Oddly enough, the two mosques that the Mughals constructed in Kashmir, the Mullah Shah Masjid and Patthar Masjid never found favour with the local population. This mosque was completely closed for worship by the Sikh and Dogra rulers. During the early part of the twentieth century, it was even used to store gunpowder (shoora). Following an agitation the mosque was handed over by the Dogras to the Muslim community in 1932. Prayers were offered here on only a couple of occasions, before it was abandoned once more. The mosque suffered some damage during the earthquake of 2005. Repairs and cleaning are presently underway.

❸ THE HAMMAM OF DARA SHIKOH

Four hammams were built during the reign of Shah Jahan at Shalimar, Achbal, Nagar Nagar and Pari Mahal. Of the four, three were built under the joint collaboration of Dara Shikoh, Jehanara Begum and Mullah Shah. The Mughal hammam developed over the centuries since Babur's reign, and had become an integral part of imperial architecture.

Mughal hammams were based on three functional units, a rakht kan (dressing room), a sard khana (cold room), and a garam khana (hot room). The rakht kan is commonly referred to as jamvar khana in Kashmir. There was no architectural norm for the shape and arrangement of these individual units. According to Ebba Koch, 'they could be anything from a single chamber to a group of interconnecting rooms.' The hammams were also provided with toilets. Unlike the Mughal hammams, the traditional Kashmiri hammam consists of a single hot room or chamber with smaller cubicles for bathing.

According to what little information is available from historical records, the palace of Dara was situated on a lower level, further to the east of the hammam, in close proximity to Kathi Darwaza, the main entrance to the city of Nagar Nagar. Interestingly, the main entrance portico of the hammam faces in this direction, rather than towards the mosque.

The hammam consists of a single-storey, linear structure aligned along the north-south axis parallel to the mosque and is made up of a series of interconnected chambers. As such it is the largest surviving Mughal hammam in Kashmir, bigger in area than the Achabal or Shalimar hammams.

As the main entrance door to the building is not located in the middle; consequently the building does not possess the typical symmetrical façade of Mughal architecture. This could be a result of site constraints. A similar entrance is located on the other façade of the building, facing the mosque.

The hammam is built of brick masonary with lime mortar. The brick used here is lakhori or badshahi, and resembles a tile of almost uniform thickness (1.5 inches), yet varying sizes. Interestingly, the mortar used is of similar thickness as the bricks. The walls were originally plastered with lime, traces of which can still be seen.

Within the building are a series of interconnected halls. The main hall is to the left of the main entrance. A stone column at the centre of this hall supports the ceiling, made up of four shallow domes. A narrow corridor links the entrance, this hall and a vaulted chamber on the opposite side, which is in turn connected to a second room. The domed chamber on the north is a rectilinear alcove that leads to the rear gateway, that opens out onto the bagh, leading to the caravanserai and mosque.

The other chamber, covered with a high bangla ceiling, originally had an

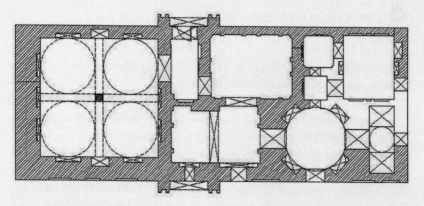

Ground plan of the Hammam of Dara Shikoh.

opening on the south, leading to a domed octagonal room which is presently blocked. The fact that this domed octagonal chamber originally had no opening indicates that it might have been used as a garam khana. A narrow passage comprising two small vaulted cubicles, on the eastern side of the octagonal room provides access to another vaulted chamber. There is another room to the immediate south of the octagonal room. Apparently this chamber and the octagonal room were connected through a narrow passage, now blocked. This small room can be accessed from outside though a separate entrance. If the octagonal chamber was the garam khana, then this room may have had the hearth to warm water and therefore required outside access. Alternatively it might have housed the toilets, with outside access for removal of waste.

A number of terracotta pipes can be seen in the building along various corner junctions. Possibly there is a similar piping system in the floor of the building, presently hidden under the earth. Excavation beneath the floor will help in uncovering such a piping system, provide clues about the location of various pools (hauz) inside the building, and also make it possible to identify the separate functions of the chambers.

The external façade of the building comprises a series of openings and blind arches on either side of the iwan, lending harmony to a building that is essentialy asymmetrical. Traces of a projecting stone chajja can be seen at the roof level. The roof also had sloping sides, as in the adjacent Mullah Shah Mosque or even in the Patthar Masjid. This is a basic departure from the traditional Mughal style of construction and seems to be the only concession that the Mughal builders made to the cold winters of Kashmir, when snow would tend to accumulate on the rooftop. The window openings in the Mullah Shah mosque are filled in by a stone jaali, based on the traditional geometric

Mullah-Shah's Disciple

Mullah Shah was born in 1584 A.D, in the village of Erkesa in Badakshan. At the age of 22 he left home and travelled, finally finding his spiritual mentor, Mian Mir.

The eldest son of the Mughal Emperor Shah Jahan, Dara was born on 20 March 1615. From an early age he was drawn to all things mystical, and on his first visit to the valley, when he was only 24 years old, as a part of the emperor's entourage (of over 100,000 people!) he met Mullah Shah. Within a year Dara was formally initiated into the Qadiri order of Sufism and his life long devotion to Mullah Shah had begun.

For many years Dara learnt Sanskrit along with his sister Jehanara. He studied the Hindu epics and read the Vedas avidly. At his command the Upanishads and the Bhagvad Gita were translated into Persian. He even presented a stone railing to the temple of Kesho Rai at Mathura, and gave full liberty to Raja Jai Singh of Jaipur, to appoint the presiding priest at the temple of Brindavan built by Man Singh. Dara's study of Hinduism and Islam had convinced him that there was no difference between the two. In his Tariqal-at-Haqiqat Dara wrote:

'Thou art in the Kaaba as well as in the Somnath Temple

In the convent as well as in the tavern

Thou art at the same time the light and the moth;

The wine and the cup, the sage and the fool;

The fiend and the stranger

Thou are thyself the rose and the amorous nightingale

Thou art thyself the moth around the light of thine own beauty'

Among his original compositions in Persian there are biographies of Muslim saints, a handbook on the Qadiriya orders, and an ambitious foray into comparative religion, Majma-ul-Baharin (meeting of the two oceans).

But the liberal religious climate created by Akbar and sustained by Jahangir and Shah Jahan, reaching a climax in the story of Dara Shikoh, had deeply offended orthodox Muslims across the empire. Rallying around Dara Shikoh's younger brother Aurangazeb, they pushed for the defeat, public humiliation and execution of Dara in 1659.

patterns prevalent through the Islamic world. It is possible that a similar jaali was also used in the hammam.

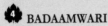 BADAAMWARI

To complete this walk, stroll around the hill to the recently renovated Badaamwari (almond orchard). This is a garden built on shallow steps that stands where the original Bagh-e-Waris-Khan stood. Waris Khan was a governor of Kashmir in Afghan times and till today you can find a well here

Almond blossoms in the month of March.

— the Waris Khan well, where it is said that the governor killed and threw his enemies. As you enter this garden, the well is on your extreme left, covered by a pavilion with a khatamband ceiling.

Different pathways in this contemporary garden have been planted with a variety of trees and bushes and are named after them, junipers, almond, palms. The main pathway culminates in an open air theatre that overlooks the Pokhribal Lake which is in turn linked through a canal to the Nageen and Dal Lakes. Entrance to the garden is ticketed, and it is maintained by the Jammu and Kashmir Bank.

Today's walk has given us an intimate glimpse of Mughal architecture and their lifestyles – from mosque to hammam to garden, all at a distance from the main city of Srinagar.

Almond

The almond is one of the oldest trees known to man. Almonds have been found in Early Bronze Age sites (3000-2500 B.C.) and even in the pyramids in Egypt! It was the Roman Empire that popularized this tree from the Mediterranean across Asia.

The Kashmir Valley is ablaze with almond blossoms in March and most almond branches are grafted on young peach roots. So the peach trunk serves as the sturdy base of the almond tree when it is heavy with fruit. It is used extensively in Kashmiri cuisine and even generously sprinkled on the kahwa (tea) in the Valley.

1 Naqshband Saheb
2 Jamia Masjid
3 Dastgeer Saheb

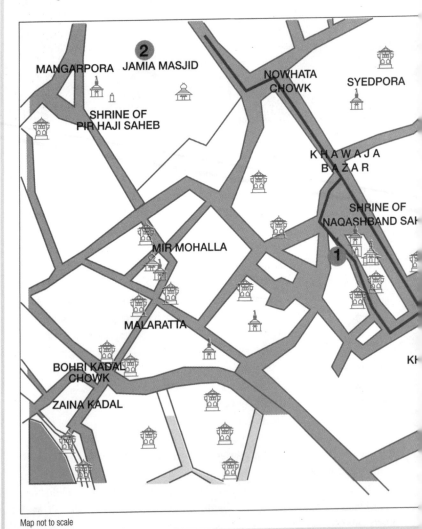

MANGARPORA   JAMIA MASJID

NOWHATA
CHOWK   SYEDPORA

SHRINE OF
PIR HAJI SAHEB

K H A W A J A
B A Z A R

SHRINE OF
NAQASHBAND SAH

MIR MOHALLA

MALARATTA

KH

BOHRI KADAL
CHOWK

ZAINA KADAL

Map not to scale

WALK 5

Of Mosques and Khanqahs

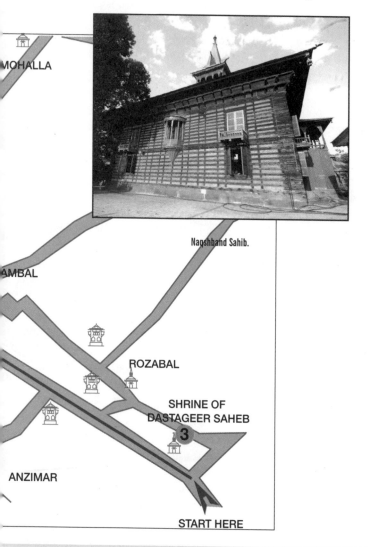

Naqshband Sahib.

MOHALLA

AMBAL

ROZABAL

SHRINE OF
DASTAGEER SAHEB

3

ANZIMAR

START HERE

Today's walk is an exploration of different expressions of the faith in the Valley. Starting from the rather severe Khanqah of Khwaja Mahmud Naqshbandi, we move onto the main mosque of Srinagar, the Jamia Masjid and finally visit the khanqah of another Sufi master, Dastgeer Saheb.

❋ 1 NAQSHBAND SAHEB

After the fall of the Chaks, the Bagh-i-Hussain Shah, which housed the palace of one of the last Kashmiri kings Sultan Hussain Shah Chak, was gifted by Emperor Shah Jahan to Khwaja Mahmud Naqshbandhi, a prominent Sufi belonging to the Naqshbandi order. Khwaja Mahmud had a khanqah built on the site in 1633, and this was the first khanqah in the Valley associated with the Naqshbandi order. Several prominent members of the Naqshbandi family are buried in a shrine opposite the khanqah. Many freedom fighters who struggled for Kashmir's independence from Dogra rule, and died on 13 July 1931 A.D., are also buried here.

The overall feel of this group of buildings, and the graveyard beyond, is one of contemplative meditation, accentuated by the deep slate grey and age old dark brown deodar wood. There is no sense of celebration here as there is in Khanqahi–i-Mualla. The different approaches to Sufism, one of silent meditation, the other of celebration are evident in the atmosphere that surrounds these two complexes.

The Naqshbandh Saheb precinct is a large complex of buildings that can be accessed through a newly constructed stone gateway on the road leading from Ranger Mohalla towards Nowhatta. From the gateway a stone paved pathway leads to the double storey shrine of Naqshband Saheb on its northern side. Immediately opposite it, on a raised stone sufa (platform), is the double storey khanqah. On the east of the khanqah, facing the road stands a newly constructed single storey building housing a hammam. Between the shrine and the khanqah on the west of the complex is the Mazar-i-Shuhda or martyrs, graveyard. The story goes

Naqshbandis are the most orthodox of all the Sufi orders. Naqshbandiyya means to 'tie the Naqsh very well.' The Naqsh is the perfect engraving of Allah's name in the heart of the murid. The Naqshbandi order, developed in north India by Ahmed al Sirhindi in the early part of the seventeenth century, was later to travel and influence the Islamic world in 1670 when Murad, a Sufi teacher from Samarkand who had studied in India, moved to live in Istanbul and later in Damascus. As the brotherhood grew, it developed into the belief that Sufism should come much closer to and strictly observe the shariat.

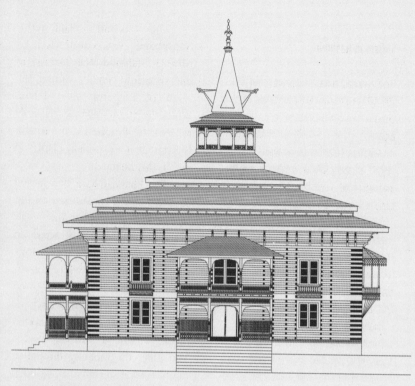

Elevation of the Khanqah of Naqshband Sahib.

that the martyrs who died battling the Dogra regime are buried here, because no one in 1931 was willing to provide burial space for the group burial of the freedom fighters as they were afraid of incurring the wrath of the Maharaja. It was Noor Shah Naqshbandi, himself a member of the freedom fighters group, who offered this ancestral graveyard. The Maharaja responded by cancelling the jagir of the Noor Shah family.

The original shrine was a square five taq building with a small porch (dhalan) opening out on the southern side. This has now been enlarged and extended along the western and northern sides of the building. The roof is double tiered and pyramidical in shape, surmounted by square pavilion (brangh) with a gabled spire on top. As you enter the aastan, the main cenotaph of the saint lies in an enclosure directly in front of you. The sanctum is covered with intricate woodwork covered with beautiful naqashi patterns. There is an elegant khatamband ceiling as well. To your left is a raised arched area, similar to a Ghulam Gardish. The west side extension can be approached through an entrance doorway on the south used by women.

Sufism in Kashmir

Sufism emerged during the Umayad period (661-700 A.D.) as a reaction to the increasing preoccupation with the material world in the expanding Muslim community across Asia and the Middle East. Kashmir served almost as a magnet, attracting Sufis of all orders through the medieval period — right from Bulbul Shah who came to Srinagar from Turkestan in 1300(approx); to Sayyid Ali Hamadani from Hamadan in Iraq in 1372; to Mohammed Amir Owaisi from Khorasan in Iran during Sultan Sikandar's reign; to the Naqshbandi order and the Qadiri sect of Mullah Shah in the period of Shah Jahan (seventeenth century).

Finding exile from possible religious persecution in their own countries, several of these Sufi masters drew a vast number of followers in the Valley. While some orders spread across different parts of India and the world (as for instance the Naqshbandias who were to impact Turkey and Syria later), others remained restricted to the Valley.

Till today the belief in and devotion of the common man to the Sufi path, the khanqahs and dargahs, has to be seen to be believed. Multitudes throng to the Sufi shrine on a holy day or even on a daily basis, to offer prayers and seek divine blessings for a newly-wed couple, an infant, a relative in pain, a new job….

The actual Khanqah-i-Naqshbandi was constructed by Khwaja Mahmud Naqshbandi in the sixteenth century during the reign of Emperor Shah Jehan. When the Moi-i-Mubarak (the holy relic of the Prophet) was brought to Kashmir, it was initially displayed within this khanqah.

The khanqah is a two-storied square building constructed on top of a raised stone platform (sufa). The building is constructed in keeping with the technology prevalent at the time, with the walls made of solid deodar logs used alternately as headers and stretchers. The space between the wooden blocks was filled with clay bricks. You enter the building through a double storey rectangular wooden portico (dhalan) centrally placed on the north, south, and eastern façade. The portico is supported on a wooden foliated arched screen, and covered by a sloping roof.

Within the building you find yourself in a double height prayer hall with a narrow linear gallery running along all four sides at the first floor level. This gallery can be accessed by a staircase from the main chamber. The ceiling is supported on four multi-faceted wooden columns with decorative wooden capitals and bases. The mehrab with its intricate wood work and glass infill is unique. The heavy wooden eaves, the cornices of the building and its construction in wood lend the building a solemn dignity.

The building has a three-tiered pyramidical roof (chaar baam) surmounted by a square open pavilion (branch) crowned with the traditional wooden

Naqshband Sahib built with deodar logs and clay bricks.

gabled spire. Hanging from the four corners of the roof cornices, just below the eaves are wooden doors, very similar in shape to the traditional earrings worn by Kashmiri women. The window openings at the first floor level, along the western façade have small projecting balconies that apparently date to the early twentieth century, and from where relics are displayed occasionally.

The building is a fine example of the traditional wooden architecture of the region, and all possible steps should be taken to preserve its original architectural character.

JAMIA MASJID

In the central section of any city with a large Muslim population, you can find a Jamia Masjid. The Jamia Masjid is a much more ambitious form of building than the neighbourhood mosque as it was built primarily for communal worship every Friday. The very word jami (from the Arabic root, means 'to assemble') and therefore Jamia Masjid everywhere are often built to accommodate hundreds, even thousands of people. Beyond prayer, a mosque is often used for religious education, sometimes mosques become places of pilgrimage (such as the Hazrat Bal in Srinagar) or for the administration of justice.

The overall feel of this group of buildings, and the graveyard beyond, is one of contemplative meditation, accentuated by the deep slate grey and age

Interior courtyard of Jamia Masjid.

old dark brown deodar wood. There is no sense of celebration here as there is in Khanqahi–i-Mualla. The different approaches to Sufism, one of silent meditation, the other of celebration are evident in the atmosphere that surrounds these two complexes.

The Jamia Masjid in Nowhatta is a wonderful example of a spacious and gracious mosque that combines the warmth of wood and brick work very successfully. Built at the end of the fourteenth century by Zain-ul-Abidin's father, Sultan Sikander, this mosque has over the centuries remained identical in plan. Among the engineers who worked on it originally were some from Khorasan in Iran. It was Budshah who built the four minars of the masjid, planted chinar trees and established a madrassa here. The mosque suffered great damage after fires in 1479 and 1674, and the Mughal Emperor Aurangzeb undertook its reconstruction. He famously asked if the chinars were safe, for a mosque can be quickly rebuilt but a full grown chinar cannot be replaced!

The mosque was closed to the public during the Sikh rule, and re-opened by Sheikh Ghulam Mohi-ud-din, the governor, who also carried out major repair work on the building. The mosque was once again repaired in 1913. The mosque is presently undergoing a phase of additions and alterations.

The huge structure contains all the design elements essential for a Kashmiri wooden building. It consists of a square courtyard of about 24 x 24 feet surrounded on all four sides by wide colonnades, the entire area being contained within a lofty exterior wall, making a rectangle of 285' sides. From

The best of all timber is that produced by the deodar. It is much in request for houses, boats and bridges, and it seems to be impervious to water. The old shrines, some of great age, are made of deodar, and the great Juma Masjid of Srinagar, is said to have been constructed of timber cut from the Tashawan Forest. The Tashawan Forest is now part of the city lying on the left bank of the river between the Fatteh and Zaina bridges. It is interesting to notice that isolated deodars are found at low elevations in many parts of the valley, where they resemble (in growth) the cedar of Lebanon. It is probable that in old days the deodar was spread all over the valley, but the building requirements of Sringar soon exhausted the deodar forests in the vicinity of the city. At present, with the single exception of the forests of the north west of the valley, there are no deodars within reach of the streams; they have all been cut either for export to the Punjab or for local use.

Walter R. Lawrence
The Valley of Kashmir

the outside what you notice is the retaining wall, with an enormous expanse of plain brickwork averaging 30 feet in height all around the building which, except for the three projecting entrances in the middle of the north, south and east, is relieved only by a series of small arched openings towards the upper portion of the building.

The main entrance on the southern side consists of a recessed portico, leading into an inner courtyard based on the traditional chaar bagh plan with a tank at the centre. The tank is mostly used for wazu by worshippers before offering prayers in the mosque. The tank was originally fed by a water channel known as Lachma-Kul, which brought water from the Sindh River into the city. The water from the tank flowed down a small ornamental stone chute, and passing out of the channel left the mosque by an underground passage in the western wall before joining the Nallah Mar canal. The water channel was closed in the 1920s. The tank is presently fed through water pipes connecting it to the municipal water lines.

The tank is constructed from well-cut dressed stone (diwar kani) with steps placed at the centre of all four sides. A fountain has recently been added to the water tank, and its inner walls are covered with blue ceramic tiles.

The court, originally planted with a series of chinars is enclosed by arches ilwains (cloisters), covered with a two-tiered sloping roof supported on an array

In the case of prominent shrines and khanqahs, the natural wooden tinge of the outer façade contrasts visually with the rich, almost sensuous internal atmosphere of the interior spaces. The dark, somber tone of natural, exposed deodar wood is often coated regularly with rogan nela thouth (copper sulphate) and resin. An admixture of dried walnut and pomegranate shells for staining add a rich brownish tinge to the wood which, due to the release of natural oils, has an inherent tendency towards acquiring a reddish tinge.

of 370 wooden deodar columns. Facing the middle of each cloister is a large entrance gateway covered with a pyramidical roof surmounted by a square open pavilion (brangh), with a spire on top. The western wall of the cloister has a black marble mehrab with beautiful calligraphic work. The upper clerestory is reached through twin staircases located in the jamb of the arch along the western façade.

The Jamia Masjid served as a principal Friday mosque for the whole of Srinagar, uptil the early twentieth century. The building is one of the best preserved examples of traditional Kashmiri architecture, which makes it absolutely essential to conserve the original character and architectural unity of this building.

DASTGEER SAHEB

Historical references show that an Afghan traveller on a visit to Kashmir presented a holy relic to the governor of the state Sardar Abdullah Khan. This belonged to the renowned Sufi saint, Syed Abdul Qadir Jeelani. The relic was deposited with Syed Buzargh Shah, a prominent Qadri Sufi of that time, and a khanqah was constructed at Khanyar in the eighteenth century from where the relic was displayed on various religious festivals. The khanqah was enlarged in the nineteenth century by Khwaja Sanaullah Shawl and is an important part of both the socio-cultural as well as the architectural vocabulary of the region.

The original khanqah consists of a linear seven taq double height building aligned along the north-west axis. The khanqah block has two octagonal double storey dubs along the corners of the main western façade dominated by an arcade of pointed arched openings. Carved eaves boards, wooden pendants, mullion work in the window openings, decorative khatamband ceiling and dedo coupled with multi-faceted deodar wooden columns are some of the main decorative features of the building. In buildings like Dastgeer Saheb, Khanqah-i-Mualla and Naqshbandh Saheb the overall ambience of the interior tend towards the gaudy in complete contrast to the building's outer appearance. This can be seen in most pan-Islamic urban architecture where a restrained and even monotonous external façade is relieved by the colourful interior.

A number of ancillary buildings have been added to the main khanqah on its northern and southern side. Immediately to the south of the double height khanqah chamber is a rectangular block which is a shrine that contains the cenotaphs of many prominent members of the Qadri Sufi order. The shrine is preceded by a two-storey block containing a mosque and a hammam.

All the buildings can be approached from a wide corridor running along the entire length of the complex on its north. Along the north-eastern corner of the khanqah there is an open pavilion covered with a multi-tiered roof, mostly used by female worshippers. The buildings seem to be in a fairly good condition, though some of the additions to the main building have cramped the physical openness associated originally with the khanqah. The main khanqah building and the shrine block are covered by a multi-tiered chaar-baam roof surmounted by a wooden dome and a spire respectively.

While the commonly held belief is that most traditional wooden shrines are made essentially of deodar with a mixture of blue pine or silver fir, yet from the account of a nineteenth-century Gazetteer it becomes clear that a variety of wood was used for different building elements, especially in the case of shrines. This includes the use of tul (mulberry) for making of shrine doors and bre (jujube) for lintels. Apparently poh (witch hazel) used to be used for rafters in buildings, where deodar was not used because of the cost involved. Traditionally, kachil (Himalayan spruce) was used for making of shingles and this would invariably have been used in shrines also.

1 Ali Kadal Bridge and Chowk

2 The Ali Kadal Chowk

3 Bulbul Lankar

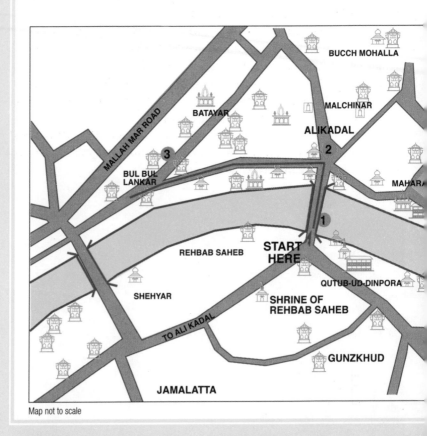

Map not to scale

WALK 6

Moving Back in Time
from Ali Kadal

The busy road of Ali Kadal today.

The road off the Ali Kadal precinct in the city core is where fourteenth century Srinagar lived and died. However, despite the historical significance of this area, a lack of conservation awareness and rebuilding over the years, has resulted in a loss of much of its original charm and character.

Yet, even today, walking in this area gives one a sense of travelling into the past, of examining the close interplay of royalty and religion in the Bulbul Shah Lankar Rinchen cenotaph off Ali Kadal.

 ## ALI KADAL BRIDGE AND CHOWK

Our first stop on this walk is the Ali Kadal Bridge, a fine example of Kashmiri trussed bridge. Originally, however, all Kashmiri bridges were cantilever bridges, where the main supports or piers were formed of layers of deodar logs resting on a foundation of uncemented stones enclosed in a triangular wooden frame. The layers were laid alternately lengthwise and across, each projecting slightly beyond the one immediately beneath it. This gave the piers the shape of an inverted pyramid, and, by reducing the distance between the piers, permitted the logs to be laid from one pier to the next one, thus forming the road. The piers were therefore strong enough to deal with the swirling flood waters below and a sufficiently heavy load of traffic above.

LIFE ALONG THE RIVER

From the riverside windows the city people can see life – busy and picturesque. Various boats of all sizes are to be seen, from the great grain barges which lie moored to the ghats to the little shell in which the Dal lake cultivator paddles his vegetables and lake-produce to market, and up and down the river paddled with many strong arms go the dungas of officials, merchants and travellers. Perhaps the daily boat up to Islamabad or down to Baramula is at last starting, if sufficient passengers have taken seats, the boat is low down in the water and each man is sitting in his neighbour's lap; or a pleasure party is starting to Manasbal, or a pilgrim boat is setting off for some shrine. The topsey-turvey bathing-boxes are full of people leisurely bathing, chattering, and gesticulating. In the winter the scene changes, the river narrows and falls, the lattice widows are covered with paper, and no one stirs out on the river except on urgent business.

Walter R. Lawrence
The Valley of Kashmir

A view of Ali Kadal Chowk.

If you look downstream (i.e., in the opposite direction to Zaina Kadal) you will see a complex of important historical buildings on the right bank of the river. Most of these are linked to the very early history of medieval Kashmir, particularly to the lives of its first Muslim King Rinchen/ Sadruddin and his own Sufi mentor, Bulbul Shah. Bulbul Shah was a widely travelled Musavi Sayyid from Turkestan, a disciple of the Surawardi School of Sufis. It is said that when he passed away, one of the pallbearers of his coffin was the very young Zain-ul-Abidin, later to become the famous Budshah of Kashmir.

This frontage on the river is therefore one of the oldest sections of the town. It is important to remember that the Jhelum was the essential artery of the city in the past as all transportation was only by water. So all major buildings came up along its banks and could initially only be accessed by boat.

Wazwan

In the valley of Kashmir, the preparation of the traditional wazwan feast is considered an art, with considerable time and effort going into it. The post of head chef or vasta waz is hereditary, moving down from father to son and many families trace their cooking skills back to the time their forefathers lived in Samarkand. The influence of Persia in cuisine can be seen in the style of food, how it is prepared and how it is served. Wan indicates a shop with an abundant supply of meat and delicacies.

Hours of planning, shopping and cooking result in the wazwan. At its most elaborate it consists of 36 different dishes. The philosophy of the wazwan is that the guests in turn must do full justice to the meal.

Look along the river's right bank to see Rinchen's mosque, followed by the shrine and mosque of Owaisi Saheb, then the building belonging to the Shahdaad family – originally Tibet baqals or those involved in trading on the Yarh and Leh Srinagar route. Just below this building is the Durga pathshala and finally Bulbul Lankar, a shrine to Bulbul Shah and the hospice. Unfortunately, however, most of these buildings have lost their original character as extensive constructions over the centuries have paid little attention to the conservation of the original architecture.

But before moving on, stop for a moment to see the varied activity on the ghats of the city. Directly below Richen's mosque, towards right, artisans can be seen washing the raw material of shawls called ruffle in the swift flowing waters of the Jhelum. (For more details on the all important shawl trade of Srinagar *see pages* 196-204). Further ahead, on yet another ghat, the huge cooking vessels of the traditional wazwans or master chefs are being washed. One can only begin to conjecture for how many hundreds of years similar activities have been taken place daily on these very ghats!

It is now time to enter Ali Kadal Chowk and walk down the road on your left with a number of historical sites located on it. Remember that you are walking a path well traversed in fourteenth-century Srinagar where the Sufi saint Bulbul Shah and his most prominent follower, the Ladakhi Prince, Rinchen Shah, who converted to Islam, lived and died.

2 THE ALI KADAL CHOWK

The Ali Kadal Chowk is one of the prominent public spaces in the old city that continues to serve as a vibrant civic plaza lined with bazaars and residences. The chowk has always been a major urban

---

Copperware

Prominent among the many shops are those that sell copperware. Copper is the preferred metal in the Valley and even though it is very expensive today, it still serves as a status symbol. Many shops that trade in copperware have been doing so for more than six generations!

Among the most distinctive of all copper vessels are the samovars used for brewing tea. This special kettle holds burning charcoal in an outer container, while the inside container holds boiling water. The samovar has travelled from the rural lands of Iran and Central Asia, also from as far away as Georgia.

Samovars come in all sizes – from a two-cup samovar to one that can hold over a hundred cups! The samovar had exquisite etching and carving all over its characteristic shape: a large rounded body, a short spout and a large curved handle. Casting samovars in copper is a traditional metal craft of Kashmir.

Other distinctive copper utensils are the trami, used to serve the wazwan feast, tash-tari for washing hands before meals and the near, a jug used for pouring water.

Residents greet each other on the bridge.

centre as it is located at the junction of the road leading from the bridge, and the main court road, serving as a secondary spine of transportation running parallel to the river.

The main chowk is dominated by the two-storied building of the Qazi Jamal-ud-din mosque with two narrow streets on either side, lined with three to four-storied residential buildings with shops on the ground floor. Many buildings still retain many of the features of traditional indigenous architecture like projecting dubs and lattice work (pinjarakari) window frames. The overall street façade serves as a cohesive linear stretch, though some of the buildings have been reconstructed. The edges of the street and main Ali Kadal are lined with a number of hawkers, making the chowk a bustling civic centre.

❸ BULBUL LANKAR

The shrine complex of Bulbul Shah was established in the year 1320-23 A.D. by Rinchen Shah, the first Muslim king of Kashmir, for his spiritual mentor, Syed Sharif-ud-din Mousi, popularly known as Bulbul Shah. Rinchen Shah had a mosque and a hospice (khanqah) constructed here, that served as the principal focal point for the newly established Muslim community. The palace of Rinchen Shah, within walking distance of the shrine complex, was

Rinchen Shah/Sadruddin

Rinchen Shah whose full name was Lhachen-r-Gyalbu-Rinchana (1322-23 A.D.) was the son of a Ladakhi chief who took over Kashmir in 1320 A.D. after the horrific pillage of the Mongols. Born and bred as a Buddhist, Rinchen embraced Islam at the hands of Bulbul Shah. Adopting the name of Sadruddin, he became the first Muslim ruler of Kashmir ruling for only a few years till he passed away in 1323 A.D, and was buried near the khanqah of Bulbul Shah.

Bulbul Shah

Syed Sharif-ud-din Mousvi commonly known as Bulbul Shah, was a disciple of Shah Niyamatullah Farsi, a saint of the Suharwardiya order of Sufis, who reached Kashmir during the reign of the Hindu king Sahadeva (1300-1319 A.D.). Traditional historical sources suggest that Bulbul Shah introduced Islam to the Valley. It was because of him that Rinchen embraced Islam, becoming the first Muslim ruler of Kashmir. Bulbul Shah passed away in 1320 A.D., and was buried near the khanqah where he had preached for the major part of this life.

converted into the first congregational (Jamia) mosque of the region. The shrine was endowed with a large amount of land, that presently houses the residential quarters of Bulbul Lankar. Both Bulbul Shah and Rinchen are buried here. However, since 1953 a number of the earlier medieval structures have been reconstructed. As a result, this area has lost both its original character as well as its physical continuity.

The first building you see is the single-storey structure serving as the shrine of Bulbul Shah. A series of steps along the outer mehrab (western) wall of the shrine leads down to the ghat. Further to the west is a small garden with a chinar tree adjoining a park, containing the cenotaph of Rinchen Shah. The mosque which used to function originally as a khanqah, lies on the main road to the north-west of the shrine. The mosque and the park containing the cenotaph of Rinchen have separate entries facing the road. As a whole the precinct area lacks a cohesive unifying architectural character, a result of the socio-political upheavals which shook the region after the fall of the Sultanate in the sixteenth century.

Today the site stands physically demarcated into three different parts: the shrine, the mosque and the park containing the cenotaph. Efforts need to be made to unite them into a single coherent unit, which could serve as a cultural landmark.

The Masjid-i-Khanqah-i-Bulbul Shah is a double-storied rectangular building in dressed stone (diwar kani) forming a part of the whole precinct. The most dominant features of the mosque are a series of pointed arched

Owaisi Saheb

A renowed Sufi saint and Persian poet, Mohammed Amir Owaisi came to Kashmir from a town in Khurasan (Iran) during the period of Sultan Sikandar. Budshah Zain-ul-Abidin's wife adopted him as one of her sons and khanqahs were built for him at Ali Kadal and Asham. In the khanqah at Ali Kadal a wooden plank is preserved as a relic of Owaisi Saheb. This mysteriously appeared in the Jhelum when Owaisi was murderously assaulted in the battle for the throne following the death of Zain-ul-Abidin, and Owaisi had predicted this would happen. The last washing of his corpse was carried out on this plank, or so the story goes.

openings and triangular gables running all along the roof edge on the southern façade. The roof is surmounted by a square pavilion (brangh) crowned by a traditional spire.

The shrine, erected on top of a stone retaining wall facing the Jhelum is a single-storied building approximately 50' x 25 feet in size. Entering the building from the north you will find the cenotaph of the saint to the left and a small space for offering prayers on your right. The main façade comprises of an arcade of five segmental arched openings, surrounded by bands of raised brick masonary. The building has a traditional pyramidical roof (chaar baam) with two square pavilions (brangh) placed along the central ridge. The central brangh is covered by a small bulbous wooden dome clad in G.I. sheets. A series of small kiosk-like features are located along the roof edge. The shrine rebuilt in 1952 hardly bears any resemblance to the original structure.

The grave of Rinchen Shah was discovered in 1890 A.D. by A.H. Francke, an archaeologist from the Moravian Mission. A park has recently been constructed around the cenotaph by the state government after removing houses that occupied the site. A raised stone plinth in diwar kani with a cement jali around it, having an arcade of maharaji bricks at the back, inscribed with the history of Rinchen Shah, is all that remains of the mausoleum of the first Muslim king of Kashmir.

APPENDICES

Srinagar in the Mughal Period

If you are interested in only visiting structures built by the Mughals in the Valley, you could create a new route which would combine walks and a drive to be able to see most of the extant buildings. The Pathar Masjid, just off the new Zaina Kadal in the old city, is the logical starting point. Built by the extremely powerful Mughal Empress Noor Jehan, wife of Jahangir, this elegant if severe mosque is built of grey limestone. For more on this particular building, *see pages* 124-25. From here you could drive up Hari Parbat, passing through either the Kathi Darwaza or Sangeen Darwaza, built by Akbar to alleviate starvation in a year of famine, 1597. It was on this hill that the imperial Mughal army was stationed, and it is said that at one time the many Mughal residences, palaces, hammams, and gardens covered most of the hillside. All that remains and that is worth seeing in detail is the Mullah Shah complex that includes a mosque, caravanserai, and hammam, described on pages 164-67.

Mughal Kashmir would be incomplete without visiting the world famous Mughal Garden that surrounds the Dal Lake. At one time access was only by water, but today you can drive down Boulevard Road to visit the neighbouring gardens of Shalimar and Nishat, extensively described on pages 154-60, and finally drive up the Zabarwan Mountain to Pari Mahal, page 161.

The Sufi Way

In the medieval period and later, many prominent Sufis from across the Middle East and Central Asia found a safe haven away from the Mongol hordes in the Kashmir Valley. Welcomed and supported by the kings of the time they rose to prominence as their followers swelled. Sufism appealed to the common man and they thronged the khaqahs in large numbers seeking support and salvation. An interesting half day can be spent at the khanqah of Shah Hamadan, Naqshbandh, Dastageer, and the mosque of Mullah Shah on Hari Parbat. The typical wood structures of the Kashmiri shrine with its three-tiered pyramidical roof, brangh and spire can be seen in all its variations, and it will also give you a chance to see Sufism as a living faith with many followers.

AALI MASJID

Five huge chinars frame the paved brick walkway to the recently renovated Aali Masjid, a conservation project carried out by INTACH. This beautiful medieval mosque is a five minute drive from the oldest section of Srinagar, and is located just off the Idgah Maidan. Even though Aali Masjid is the second largest mosque in Srinagar, second only to the Jamia Masjid, other than a brief description in the Gazetteer of 1872; the building has been ignored by all those who have written about the architecture of Kashmir.

The Aali Masjid is linked historically to the Khanqah-i-Mualla (Shah Hamadan Complex) that was our starting point for Walk One. It is said that Ali Hamadani's son – Mir Syed Mohammed Hamadani – bought or was bestowed with the land, on which Aali Masjid now stands, during the reign of Zain-ul-Abidin's elder brother Ali Shah. Hence the name Aali Masjid. But this is only one possible interpretation and historians have yet to come to a definitive conclusion about how and when Aali Masjid came to be built. Another plausible explanation is that the popular Mughal governor of Kashmir, Ali Mardan Khan built it in 1650-1657, hence the name. Also Emperor Jahangir's governor Islam Khan had further work done on Aali Masjid in 1664, possibly enclosing the original deodar columns within masonary walls. The chinar trees we see in the forecourt were probably planted at that time as well. During the Afghan period the masjid caught fire and was gutted and in 1801 an Afghan governor, the

Lattice Work

Framing openings in latticework – cut into elaborate geometric or vegetal forms – has been an appealing element of Indian architecture. Whether in stone, wood or stucco the jaali or pinjrakari adorns buildings as contemporary as Corbousier's Chandigarh, or the windows of a nineteenth century middleclass Kashmiri home, or even the dargah of Salim Chisti in medieval Fathepur Sikri. This trellis work is not only practical, allowing cooling breezes to enter the enclosed space in summer and warm breezes in winter, but also affords a sense of privacy, particularly for Muslim women. The light that filters through a lattice work screen is constantly fluid – whether sunlight at day, or lamplight at night. In the Mughal era architects and stone cutters created latticework in a great variety of pattern, shape, and size. While the jaalis at Akbar's Fathehpur Sikri are ruggedly geometric, Jahangir's are much more delicate while Shah Jahan preferred arabesques and floral motifs.

The recently renovated Aali Masjid.

prominent Sardar Governor Gul Mohammed Khan, renovated the mosque once more.

It was in 1935, under the supervision of the Archaeological Survey of India (ASI), that the present three-tiered pyramidical roof with exposed wooden trusses came into being. The wooden lattice windows were replaced by glass shutters and a raised wooden floor created in the main prayer hall in 1985.

The usual function of an Idgah is to be large enough to allow for the massive congregational prayers on the occasion of the two festivals of Id that are celebrated across the Muslim world. It is rare for an Idgah maidan to have a building. However, the severe Kashmir winter with several inches of snow would make outdoor prayer impossible. A covered structure was therefore essential, and as the years went by, it became larger and larger as the number of believers grew.

During the early part of the twentieth century the Id sermons were given from the mosque while the Id namaz was offered in the open field of the Idgah. According to locals the rectangular platform projecting at the centre of the southern façade of the mosque was used by Mirwaiz Yousuf Shah, a prominent

Aali Masjid as seen from the back.

religious preacher, for delivering the Id khutba (sermon). The mosque also served as a rallying point for the freedom movement against Dogra rule in the early part of the twentieth century.

Aali Masjd is surrounded by open land on three sides, with the main Idgah ground to the south of the mosque. Towards the south western corner of the Idgah a small graveyard (Mazar-i-Shouda) has been carved out, where some prominent Kashmiris who died during the political turmoil of the early 1990s, lie buried.

A double-pillared porch of deodar wood pillars with stone carved bases forms the imposing frontage of Aali Masjid. As you face the entrance way, two parallel staircases lead to the upstairs gallery. The central door opening is accessed from a raised stone platform covered with a wooden balcony (dub), supported on wooden columns.

As you enter the space below you find yourself in a large rectangular hall with 156 pillars, directly facing the simple mihrab.

Aali Masjid is a hypostyle mosque, a style that emerged first in Iraq, a building with a roof resting on rows of columns. Add more columns and the space can be enlarged, without affecting the original structure. This style dominated Islamic architecture around the world from 715 A.D. to the tenth century, and was often copied later.

The underlying principle of a hypostyle hall is the basic unit, usually square in shape defined by four columns which are the main structural supports. So a large prayer hall, a functional requirement for Muslim worship, could easily be constructed by building multiples of such units.

In the case of Aali Masjid, the basic structure is a 12 x 12 feet grid supported on 15 feet tall wooden columns. The main hall on the ground floor measuring 200.75 x 67.26 m consists of 75 such modules. There are fifteen aisles perpendicular to the qibla wall, so the space is defined by five rows of wooden columns.

An interesting feature of the building is the presence of window openings on the qibla wall. Normally this wall is constructed without any window opening, or the openings, if provided, are located above the line of vision, and are mostly in the nature of clerestory windows.

The overall feel within the hall, with its plain white walls, is a sombre, almost monastic atmosphere accentuated by the lofty wooden colonnade. One hardly finds traces of the rich warm tones traditionally associated with the Muslim architecture of Kashmir whether it is the exquisite papier-mâché, the rich khatambandh or the earthly tone of mud plastered walls. Probably one of the reasons for this lies in the repair work carried out over the years. Entering the building hundred years ago would have been totally different when the windows were filled with beautiful pinjrakari work, filtering sunlight through the intricate openings, bringing a nuanced everchanging light into the shadowy interior. The replacement of these windows by glass shutters in 1985 robbed the building of one of its most important architectural elements, an element that places the building within its local building tradition. Today, once again, there are latticework windows. Delicate pinjrakari filters the light into the rather massive interior, and more light pours in from the two skylights on the first floor.

The repairs have also resulted in the loss of another essential Kashmiri architectural feature, the roof. Traditionally Kashmiri roofs known as burza pash consisted of a low-lying pitched roof covered with burza (layer of birch bark) as a water proofing material. The layer of bark would be covered with soil that was in turn planted with a variety of bulbs including tulips, daffodils, and narcissus. The bloom of these flowers on the rooftop from spring onwards gave a unique look to the city over the centuries. It was only in the beginning of the twentieth century that these traditional roofs were replaced with corrugated G.I. sheet roofs, losing their attractive, ecologically rich character. Amongst the earliest monumental buildings whose roofs were replaced were Jamia Masjid, Naqshband Saheb, and Aali Masjid.

The recent conservation project initiated by INTACH, focussed on correcting the various inappropriate interventions carried out over the years.

CRAFT TRADITIONS IN THE VALLEY

Working in very modest surroundings – a small crowded workshop in the old city of Srinagar or an open room in the lush countryside that surrounds the city, the Kashmiri crafts people create works of great beauty in wool, silk, wood, metal, and paper. This is a tradition that has been in existence over hundreds of years, the skills being transferred traditionally only from father to son, but now many women are involved as well. Working through most of the day in silent concentration, the artistry of the crafts people of the Valley is known across the world.

In this section you will find some information on three of the many crafts practised in Srinagar the shawl, wood carving and papier-mâché.

THE SHAWLS

Through most of the world, the word cashmere itself suggests the shawl. The shawl's identification with the valley it was nurtured in is as inextricable as its complex relationship with history. Over 500 years many layers of its symbolism have been trapped in its warp and weft, and there are many stories hidden in the folds of the shawls.

The Kashmiri shawl was the mainstay of the Valley's economy from approximately 1600 to 1860, over two hundred and fifty years. It was a luxury textile, patronized by the Mughal, Afghan, Sikh, and Dogra dynasties that ruled Kashmir successively. At its peak in 1861 for example it generated a revenue of £459,441. Eighty per cent of the shawls that were exported went to France, 10 per cent to America and only one per cent to Great Britain It was the imitation shawls manufactured in the Scottish town of Paisley that had a strong negative impact on the production of the Kashmiri shawl in the Valley. But the shawl was not dependant only on a European market because, by the nineteenth century, it was popular in princely courts and

For the grass you have just eaten, oh goat
Give us some good pashm
For the water you have just drunk, oh goat
Give us some good pashm
Sit down on the grass and be still, oh goat
So that we can take out your pashm
Song of the Changpo nomads of Ladakh

commercial cities all over South Asia.

High grade pashmina shawls are made of the fleece of a Central Asian species of mountain goat. This fleece grows beneath the goat's outer hair to keep it warm during the harsh cold winter and is shed during the summer.

This very fine, soft, short, flossy underwool is called Keli phumb or the pashm of the kel or shawl-goat, which is a variety of caprahircus. These goats inhabit the elevated regions of Tibet. The higher the goats live, the finer and warmer is their wool. There are several varieties of pashm according to the districts

A carpet seller displays his wares.

in which it is produced but the best comes from Changthong and Turfan. The pashm of Turfan is from goats in the Tien-shan mountains and the principal marts of collection are Turfan and Uch-turfan. Before the closure of the road to Leh by the Chinese, it used to come by caravan by the Kashgar-Yarkand-Leh route. Those who traded in this commodity were called Tibet-baqals.

It was from Ladakh that pashm made its way to Kashmir through regulated trade whose nature was specially outlined in international treaties between the various governments associated with it. The Ladakhi Arghons and the Kashmiri Tibet-baqals were engaged in the pashm trade. The Kashmiri traders with dealings in Kashgar and Yarkand mostly dealt in carpets, precious stones and other luxury goods. The Yarkandi traders had to their name three major sarais in Leh and one in Srinagar. In the early nineteenth century, Yarkand had emerged as a major stop for the trade caravans from Kabul, Badakashan, Bukhara and other surrounding areas. The availability of a rich clientele also

To what extent this shawl trade impacted the economic life of the people of Kashmir can be readily gauged by the fact that, 'all Kashmir and its wife were in the last century busy in amassing handsome fortunes in the shawl trade and the shawl merchants became so rich and luxurious as to put milk in place of water in their

An embroiderer at work.

hookahs,' wrote S. Pandit Anand Koul in *Kashmir Shawl Trade*, East and West, January 1915.

attracted the interest of many prominent Kashmiri merchants whose route to Yarkand lay through Ladakh. For most of the nineteenth century, Yarkand, along with Amritsar and Calcutta, remained the main trade centres of export for the Kashmiri traders.

... At this time (September to early November) the Leh bazaar becomes full of all sorts and conditions of men-the fair Yarkandi, jostling the slit eyed Tibetan, the Kulu men or his neighbour from Lahol doing business with men from Baltistan, Kashmir and most provinces of Northern India. And what do all these folks bring? From the North comes the Yarkandi with carpets of garish colours, furs of snow leopard, fox and wolf, stone martin and beaver. Khotan silks and thick felt mats... many of the Yarkandis combine religion and business, coming over the passes in the late summer of the year, and going via Bombay to Mecca ... the Tibetan who has brought salt, borax and Lahsa tea to barter with the Balti for dried apricorts and cooking butter. The nomad from Changthang brings the long soft wool from his long haired sheep which the Kashmiri trader carries down to be transformed into pashmia the basis of the far famed delicate cashmere shawls ... the man from Kulu had carried kerosene up here, and perhaps also china cups, whilst the merchant from India supplies German cloth or rich stuffs for the Ladaki gala dresses, chemises and pantloons, harberdashery of all kinds, Indian tea, spices, cigarettes, and the hundred and one things which are needed by Ladakhi housewife to keep her family upto the standard of civilization locally attained ...

– *Himalayan Tibet and Ladakh,* A. Reeve Herber and Kathleen M. Herber, 1903

The Tibet-baqals exchanged their raw wool for manufactured shawl goods and sold them for profit in the various markets of Central Asia, from where they were carried to Beijing and beyond.

The pashmina shawl is expensive because everything is done by hand, right from gathering the wool to weaving the yarn. All over the city, including islands on the Dal Lake, you can see young women bent low, cleaning and sorting pashm – the little balls of wool they buy by the gram in pashm markets in the old city. These they then dexterously weave into the fibre that will later go onto the loom. The hair of the kel goat is only 14-19 cms in diametre and therefore cannot be spun by machines. The production of a single pashmina shawl requires about 24 ounces of wool, obtained from four goats.

The shawl weaver labours patiently for months on a primitive loom, where two sticks support the warp on the loom, and the weft is entirely worked by the human hand. The slow process of weaving brings neatness to the finished shawl. The Kashmir state over the centuries monopolized the wool from the mountain gatherers, which was then sold to the weavers of the Valley.

Over a period of 300 years the successive rule of the Mughals, Afghans, Sikhs and Dogra left an indelible impression on the Kashmiri shawl. According to legend, during the rule of Zain-ul-Abidin a gift of woven Ladakhi wool called putto (woven from goat's wool) was presented as a gift to the king. Softer and warmer than any other covering, this developed over the next few years into the 'pashima' wool shawl.

It was the Mughals who encouraged and patronized the arts, continuing Abidin's legacy. The introduction of weavers from eastern Turkestan by Akbar, expanded the shawl output and initiated improvements in fibres and dyes.

> The shawl is a symbol of Kashmir's cultural lifestyle. Pashmina has always meant security for the women of Kashmir. In the old days women got saris of pashmina in their trousseau, but they only wore everyday wool at home. If they fell upon bad days they cut up a shawl length of pashmina and sold it to the shawl peddler for cash. Never forget, these shawls are equals to gold.
> **Sudha Koul**
> *The Tiger Ladies*

Stylised nature and the glory of the Indian paisley buta are splendidly reflected in the Kashmiri shawl, where embroidery and weaving were combined. Chain, stem and darning stitches, worked together in a style similar to Persian silm embroideries, were amalgamated with the kani shuttle weaving akin to the twill tapestry technique of Europe, with tojlis or floating bobbins inserting the patterned weft threads through the warf.

As designs and variations in colour became more complicated, with many different motifs and colours incorporated into one shawl, different pieces were woven on different looms and then linked together by the rafugar with darn stitch embroidery of incredible fineness.

The subtlety and skills and superb artistry of the extraordinary pieces of matching jamawar cloths, can be seen in the miniatures of Mughal courtiers of the time, or gauged by Willam Moorcroft's account of a shawl made up of a mind-boggling 1,500 separate pieces! In their heyday, Kashmiri dyers produced a colour range of over 300 different shades of yarn for the pattern makers to choose from. An amusing example of their ingenuity and search for perfection is that, lacking a certain green, they boiled down an English baize billard table top to achieve it!

Laila Tyabji

With Emperor Akbar showing such enthusiasm, Kashmiri shawls became an integral part of the apparel of the nobles of the country. He himself boasted of a large collection. Each piece in his wardrobe or Toshikhana was labelled with its price, date, colour, and weight. Under the Mughals, the number of shawl looms, at one time, was estimated at 40,000. In Mughal times, according to Moorcraft, 300 tints were in regular use, later reduced to 64, most of which were vegetable dyes. With Mughal patronage, artisans found outlets in markets ranging from Iran to the Indian subcontinent and beyond. The Kashmiri shawl became the universal symbol of aristocracy across the Indo-Persian world.

The European connection with the Kashmiri shawl began in 1787 when the ambassadors of Tipu Sultan of Mysore gifted them to men of rank in the Paris government. Wearing a Kashmiri shawl, Napoleon's Empress Josephine created a fashion trend throughout Europe that lasted well into the early twentieth century. She patronized a particular design and ordered it directly from Kashmir. It was delivered to her in all colours, and it is still known as the 'Josephine design' amongst Kashmiri village artisans 220 years later!

Men working together in karkhana.

Over the centuries Kashmiri artisans experimented to create a number of different techniques and designs. The distinctive kani technique using tujj or spikes at the end of which different coloured yarn were placed, is similar in some ways to textiles of Central Asia and certain Persian kilims. Pure embroidered shawls first made their appearance in the mid-nineteenth century as embroidered copies of the loom patterned or kani shawls. Later in the nineteenth century the embroidered shawl had created its own unique design vocabulary usually using end borders or delicate jaalis (lattice work) across the body of the shawl rendered in pale colours.

By the late eighteenth century in their constant search for the raw material from which to manufacture the extremely lucrative Kashmiri shawl, Kashmiri merchants began to travel as far as Chinese Turkestan, establishing warehouses in Yarkand and Khotan. Simultaneously French and British merchants began travelling to the Valley, carrying new designs and pumping money into the economy.

The shawls of Kashmir first appeared in Britain, when officials of the East India Company brought them back. The arrival of these shawls created a

During the Sikh period, the Russian Prince Alexix Soltykoff wrote of his visit to Amritsar in 1842: 'we only walked on Kashmir shawls and while sitting down I perceived that all the alleys, ceilings and streets, as far as the eye could encompass were covered with superb shawls – even the horses were prancing on them.'

sensation in the world of fashion. Here they became essentially a ladies' garment, unlike in Kashmir where they were worn by men. A lady draped in a delicate Kashmiri shawl attained the height of fashion. Seeing the growing demand back home, the East India Company, with its uncanny business-sense decided to import the shawls. With the increase in European demand, shawl workshops in the city of Srinagar increased from 12,000 in 1783 to 24,000 in 1813. But as they were neither able to meet this huge demand nor bring down the high prices, the idea of imitating the Kashmiri shawl in England itself emerged.

Towards the end of the eighteenth century traders from both England and France attempted to import Tibetan goats, Kashmiri weavers and their design vocabulary. Goats were even transported to European farms where they perished. But while their wool is essential to make the shawl, Europeans attempted to come up with a viable substitute combining wool, silk and cotton. However the warmth, light weight and fine texture of the original Kashmiri shawl proved to be impossible to imitate.

It was in Paisley, a small town near Glasgow in Scotland, that the weaving of imitation Kashmiri shawls was introduced. Paisley already had a well-established weaving industry employing about 12,000 members. It soon became the main centre for producing cheap versions of Kashmiri shawls. As the weavers of Paisley excelled in weaving the almond pattern, their shawls turned out to be a big hit in the West. Soon the motif that had originally travelled all the way from Kashmir came to be known as the Paisley motif!

The Paisley fashion wave eventually reached working-class women, who were unable to afford woven Paisleys, so printed Paisleys came into being. Printers did such a fine job that from a distance of a few feet it was hard to differentiate a cheap printed Paisley from a more expensive woven one. The once exclusive Paisley shawls became so common that the elite, who govern the world of fashion, decided to switch to a new fashion.

To break the monopoly of the British East India company trade, the French General Alland in Ranjit Singh's court actively supported the shawl trade and its

export to France. An album of delicate tracings of Kashmiri Shawls and their designs chosen to appeal to France tastes, appeared in Chavant's design book in 1837 *Album de Cashemirien* by the Kashmiri editor Kel-Arak-Oghlon (possibly supported by Alland). Alland's successor, Venture continued with this active interest in trade and introduced another Frenchman, Le Bouef who established himself in the shawl business in Srinagar.

As the shawl trade dominated the Kashmir economy, the Dogra rulers established the Dagh-Shawl, a department that attempted to control and extract taxes at every stage of the manufacture of every shawl. Duties were imposed on the import of pashm, on the dyeing, even on the completion of every single line of embroidery! These taxes became so oppressive that the ordinary shawl worker was paying five rupees out of every seven he earned to the state. Compounding their misery, the distribution of susidized grain was also limited to shawl manufacture.

> In bittered despairing mood, the shawl bafs made a wooden bier, such as the Muslims use to carry their dead to the place of internment. Placing a cloth over the coffin, they carried it to and from the procession, exclaiming, Raj Kak is dead, who will give him a grave?'
>
> – *Kashmir Misgovernment* by Robert Thorpe (regarding the April 1865 Rebellion against the Dagh Shawl Deptartment headed by the Hindu Pandit, Raj Kak)

In spite of this tax, the Kashmiri shawl industry prospered toward the end of the nineteenth century with the increasing European demand for these prized articles of fashion.

As a result the shawl traders ruled the roost and it was through them and the tremendous demand for their luxury product, that the state stayed afloat. The percentage of their profit was typically 500 per cent. By 1871 shawls worth 28 lakh rupees were exported! As a result those in charge of the shawl manufacturing units strongly influenced the economy of this state, as the sale of shawls brought in more money than the entire land revenue of the state!

> By 1890, the state withdrew entirely, abolishing the department of the Dagh-Shawl. 'The manufacture, which formerly brought half a million a year into Kashmir, is now well nigh moribund. Unless means are taken by the Government to preserve it, the art of weaving the finest shawl will probably be extinct fifteen to twenty years hence. The warehouses of London and Paris are full of shawls which find no purchasers, and the value in Kashmir has consequently fallen to a third of what it was ten years ago.
>
> – The Indian Catalogue of the Colonial and Indian Exhibition, 1886

The decline of the powerful class of shawl merchants was to have a huge impact on the socio-economic landscape of late nineteenth and early twentieth century in Kashmir. They began to battle for political and religious space in the Valley as they managed many of the religious shrines here.

PAPIER-MÂCHÉ

Papier-mâché refers to the art of creating objects from mashed and moulded paper pulp. In Kashmir these objects are traditionally painted and covered by a layer of varnish.

The art of making pen cases from mashed paper (kar-i-kalamdan) was known in Seljuk Iran, from where it spread to other parts of Central Asia in the medieval period. It was from Samarkand that Zain-ul-Abidin obtained artisans well versed in the art. Most historical records show that the craft was only practiced in the capital, Srinagar and that too within the Shia community; most of whom were immigrants from Persia.

Over the centuries papier-mâché continued to be patronized getting a fillip when French agents operating in the Valley began to pack the shawls that were sent from Kashmir to France in papier-mâché boxes. Once they had reached France these boxes were sold separately; fetching a high price. Soon these papier-mâché objects carved out a separate market for themselves across Europe. Gradually along with boxes, papier-mâché flower vases were also in demand.

The extent of the French influence on the local Kashmiri artisan can be gauged from the fact that the term 'papier-mâché' replaced the traditional name of the craft in its native place as well.

The basic material from which papier-mâché objects were traditionally made was paper and cotton rags, mashed into pulp. But over the years pine and fir wood replaced paper pulp. The advantage of wood over paper pulp was the ability to manufacture articles with

A papier-mâché artist at work.

clean, clear and straight edges. In the course of the twentieth century cardboard (ghata), also began to be used as it was inexpensive.

The craft has now evolved into a distinctive form of surface decoration (naqashi) applied over an object made completely from paper pulp or employing at least one layer of paper. So the term papier-mâché today means the technique and process of surface decoration rather than the composition of the object which is to be decorated. However, the actual painting or naqashi is always applied over a layer of paper.

The art of naqashi is the final stage of a highly evolved process, that starts with the making of the object (saakhta), the preparation of the surface, the selection of the requisite design pattern (naqsh or tarah) and colours to be used. All the different stages of the production process are streamlined; employing skilled craftspeople. The skills involved are passed on orally from one generation to the next.

The traditional motifs and designs painted on the object distinctly reflect the rich flora and fauna of the Kashmir valley. Other than the chinar leaf and almond (paisley) motif that appear in all Kashmiri craft objects whether woven, embroidered or made in wood, the typical motifs in papier-mâché include the rose, iris, gul-i-wilayat, carnation, tsunth posh (apple blossom), gul-i-lala, gulal (poppy), pamposh (lotus), yambirzal (narcissus), and nargis (daffodil).

Various motifs are also intermingled to create new patterns. The designs may be spread all over the surface (without an apparent beginning or end) or are repeated (mostly in form of medallions) or used as a border (hashiya). Figurative representation can be seen of court scenes (durabar), animal hunts (jungle tarah), historic epics or scenes from Umar Khayam's Rubiyatt.

A unique feature of Kashmiri papier-mâché is the delicate shading obtained by very fine brush work, almost in the manner of fine semi-curvilinear brush work, and is known as partaz. The same technique is also employed to fill in small gaps in the background between various motifs. In fact barring the base coat, which is done with broad vertical strokes, most of the rendering in Kashmiri papier-mâché is done with small circular or semi-circular brush strokes. The motifs are delineated with fine, uniform lines.

Traditionally most of the colours used in papier-mâché were mineral, organic or vegetable based. White was obtained from a local stone called shali kani, yellow (zard) from Gul-i-Ksu (flower) and weflangil (wild plant). Black from burnt and pounded cow dung or by burning pomegranate peels, red from cochineal, lin (forest wood) and saffron, ultramarine from yarkand and white lead from Russia. Today poster colours are mostly used.

Till late nineteenth century traditional colours were used: crimson, green, and blue with the occasional use of black. Within an object the colour scheme was limited to four or five basic colours, in a variety of shades giving the effect, from a distance of an abundance of different colours.

When the object made either by hand or on a mould reaches the naqash it is first covered with thin paper strips that act as a barrier between the plaster covering the object and the paintwork, ensuring that the painted surface does not crack. Earlier muslin was also used along with kashur kakaz (local hand-made paper).

The surface is then covered with a base coat of paint and the required design is outlined on the surface by pencil. This is known as khat travun. Originally master craftspeople would draw out the khat without the help of any stencil or khakha. But these days many younger artisans prefer to make use of khakas, perforated paper stencils. Rubbing the khaka with chalk leaves a faint mark on the surface that has to be painted. These faint lines are generally outlined with zarda or yellow. Filling colour within the motif is known as aastar. In case some portions of the work are to be raised (or embossed) a process known as vathlavun is followed. After the object has been painted it is covered with two coats of varnish to give the required glossy finish. Formerly, resins obtained from the tree known locally as sundaris (copal) were used in this process. If the painted surface is to be highlighted with gold; it is applied after the first coat of varnish and is then covered with another coat of varnish.

Painting was traditionally done with locally made brushes using goat or ass's hair, and for minute details brushes made from a cat's tail were used. The gold outlining of motifs is also done with the same brushes, though some artists have begun using pen nibs.

Traditionally, papier-mâché objects used to be defined on the basis of size:
• Masnadi: small, transportable boxes, which could be carried on the person.
• Farshi: larger, bulkier objects used to be made which include the boxes ordered by French shawl merchants for storing their shawls.

Papier-mâché was also used for interior decoration with ceilings, wall panels and doors decorated by a final layer of painted papier-mâché. The oldest surviving papier-mâché work in building interiors can be traced to the nineteenth century, both in shrines, as well as in private residences.

The average earning of a naqash can vary from 3000 to 10,000 rupees a month, depending on the craftsmanship and the number of hours spent every day.

An elaborately carved walnut wood exterior of a houseboat.

WALNUT WOOD CARVING

Using locally fabricated hand tools, the Kashmiri wood carver delicately creates motifs that have evolved over the centuries. The wood that he works with is walnut wood. The wood of the walnut tree is hard, dense, finely grained and can be polished to a very smooth finish. It is immensely popular for the making of furniture, utility items, and art objects. Kashmir valley is the only area in India where the walnut tree grows. The colour of the wood ranges from creamy white to dark chocolate. Air-dried walnut wood becomes a rich purplish-brown, while kiln-dried wood tends to be a dull brown colour.

In the nineteenth century, European demands for cabinets, tables, boxes, and trays and even guns saw a boom in this wooden craft industry. A resurgence of the same was seen with the revival of Indian handicrafts in the 1950s.

The master craftsman (wasta or naqash) uses calculated measured strokes for chipping, carving and rounding of the surface of the wood. The entire process is very similar to the art of stone sculpture (shilpi). His lexicon is a host of motifs, stylized forms of the varied flora and fauna of the region. This fascination for intricate detail developed in the latter part of the nineteenth century under European influence, when the bold woodcarving of yesteryears was replaced by a highly complex process of cutting.

Kashmiri walnut woodcarving is practiced in five main styles:

Undercut *(Khokerdar)*: This type of carving, highly reflective of traditional stone carving, usually consists of multi-layers that can go upto seven (satnarey). The overall effect is a three-dimensional depiction of various motifs, with their edges rounded off. This style is usually carried out on panels and is a favourite with many established craftspeople. The images are taken from a jungle, including deer, bears, snakes, parrots, and various form of foliage.

Open or Lattice work *(Jallidahr, Shabokdhar)*: A favourite with artisans working on screens with beautiful see-through jaalli work. Chinar leaf motifs are often used

Walnut wood carver and his wares.

and also employed especially in items of furniture like the backs of chairs.

Deep Carving *(Vaboraveth)*: This style gives the impression of being raised from the surface and the designs are mainly dragons or the lotus motif.

Engraved Carving *(Padri)*: Usually this type of work comprises of thin panels along the rim of the surface with perhaps a central motif.

Shallow Carving *(Sadikaam)*: This type of carving is normally employed all over a flat surface.

The Kashmiri walnut woodcarver never uses geometrical patterns which are basically associated with khatamband (fir wood ceilings) and pinjarkari (wooden lattice work screens).

During the Mughal period, inlay work of metal in walnut wood was also widespread; but the art died over the centuries. The walnut wood industry suffered a decline during the Afghan and Sikh period before staging a revival during Dogra rule, when articles of furniture especially chairs and tables were manufactured especially for European markets.

Walnut wood carving is largely practiced in Srinagar city. Till today the industry is largely limited to the production of those items that were being made in the nineteenth century and they still command a high price.

MOTIFS

The prominent motifs that are used in walnut wood carving are:

Gul Tarah *(Flower motif)*: This design uses various flowers in a stylized version. They may be represented individually, as a bouquet or in the form of a plant with branches.

Phulay Tarah *(Blossom motif)*: Depictions of almond, peach, apple, pear, cherry, and saffron blossoms mostly.

Kandh Posh Dhar *(Flowers with thorns)*: This design uses a rose motif along with the branches and thorns.

Gass-i-tarah *(Grass)*: This is the grass, mostly of water plants and reeds.

Mavi Dahar *(Fruit bearing trees)*: Fruits like apple, pear, walnut etc. with or without the tree.

Dach Tarah *(Grape motif)*: One of the most popular motifs in wood carving, as well as papier-mâché, depicting grapes along with the leaves and vine.

Badam Tarah *(Almond motif)*: The almond is rendered in this design in a stylized manner similar to that employed in shawls.

Bhoni Tarah *(Chinar motif)*: The chinar leaf pattern, one of the most popular motifs in the market.

Janavar ti Jandhar Tarah *(Animal motif)*: This design depicts various birds, animals and aquatic animal species. These include bulbul, parrot, hoopoe, dove, pigeon, mynah, sparrow, crow, golden oriole, duck, geese, fish, lion, deer, rabbit, horse, snake, goat etc, mainly those animal and bird species that are found in Kashmir.

Shikar Gah *(Hunt scenes)*: A favourite design mostly used for undercut wood carving depicting hunt scenes with a king mounted on an elephant or horse along with his entourage.

Darbar Dhar *(Court scenes)*: This design depicts court scenes, along with Persian or Kashmiri couplets.

Jang Dar *(War scenes)*: This design depicts scenes of battle.

Harfi Dhar: This is based on carving of Arabic, Persian, or Kashmiri verses.

Chand Chutahi Dhar: This design involves a central motif (chand) on a plane surface with four motifs along the corner (chutahi).

Raiz Kari: This is the depiction of intricate floral work.

Pura Kar *(Full work)*: In this design the whole surface is covered with dense floral patterns.

INDEX

SELECT BIBLIOGRAPHY

Bernier, Francois, *Travels in the Mogul Empire*, CUP, New York, 2011.

Dughlat, Muhammad Haider, *The Tarikh-i-Rashidi of Mirza Muhammad Haider Duglat: A History of the Moghuls of Central Asia*, Sampson Low, Marston and Company, London, 1895.

Edwardes, Michael, *Bound to Exile: Victorians in India*, Sidgwick & Jackson, London, 1969.

Haksar, A.N.D., *The Courtesan's Keeper: A Satire from Ancient Kashmir*, Rupa, New Delhi, 2009.

Hodgson, Marshall G.S., *Rethinking World History: Essays on Europe, Islam and World History*, CUP, New York, 1993.

Koul, Sudha, *The Tiger Ladies: A Memoir of Kashmir*, Beacon Press, Massachusetts, 2002.

Lawrence, Sir Walter, *The Valley of Kashmir*, Asian Educational Services, 1895.

Welch, Stuart Cary, *Imperial Mughal Painting*, University of Michigan, 1978.

Zutshi, Chitralekha, *Languages of Belonging: Islam, Regional Identity and the Making of Kashmir*, OUP, New York, 2004.